✳ new york's 50+ best places to enjoy dessert

By Andrea DiNoto and Paul Stiga

universe publishing

ACKNOWLEDGMENTS

We wish to thank the tipsters who led us to great dessert destinations, the tasters who contributed yeas and nays, the experts who kept computers humming and clarified pastry terms, and all those who shared dessert-eating stories, among them: Terry Ackerman, Anna Teresa Callen, Frank Farnham, Elizabeth Guinsberg, Michael Guinsberg, Nancy Nicholas, Grace Young, Jeanyee Wong, and special thanks to Linda Hetzer, who helped immeasurably with cake walks and research, and who contributed the Vegan Sidebar on page 84.

First published in the United States of America in 2003
by UNIVERSE PUBLISHING
A Division of Rizzoli International Publications, Inc.
300 Park Avenue South
New York, NY 10010
www.rizzoliusa.com

© 2003, 2008 by Andrea DiNoto and Paul Stiga
Cover design by Paul Kepple and Jude Buffum @ Headcase Design
www.headcasedesign.com
Cover illustration by Mary Lynn Blasutta
Interior design by Susan Van Horn for Headcase Design
Typesetting by Tina Henderson

2008 2009 2010 2011 2012/10 9 8 7 6 5 4 3 2 1
Distributed by Random House
Printed in the United States of America
ISBN: 978-07893-1799-5
Library of Congress Catalog Control Number: 2007910367

Publisher's Note
Please note that while every effort was made to ensure accuracy at the time of publication, it is always best to call ahead to confirm that the information is still up-to-date.

contents

introduction

Openings. Closings. Expansions. Relocations. Name changes. Chef changes. Menu changes. This is New York. And just because a place is a great place to enjoy dessert doesn't mean it will be there the next time you look for it—or that what you find will be the same. So we've done the looking for you and come up with this completely revisited and revised edition of *New York's 50+ Best Places to Enjoy Dessert*.

Our conclusion: The variety of choices is greater than ever. The level of imagination is higher. The quality is as good as it's ever been—or better. Truly. And there is a reason.

As competition for your dining dollar has grown—dining out and taking out are huge in New York these days—desserts have become a fresh way for competitors to distinguish themselves from the pack.

Many content themselves with perfecting the ultimate, *echt* chocolate cake, mousse, or tiramisu.

Some constantly reinvent their offerings, using artisanal finds and seasonal bounty.

More and more dazzle with choice, with dessert "events" and weekend dessert brunches.

And the most adventurous are combining unexpected flavors and turning to main-course ingredients (think mustard, edamame, and arugula) to create new sweet sensations.

All that energy—along with ever more talented new chefs committed to making their mark in this special world—makes New York the #1 dessert destination in the world.

About the restaurants in this guide:

Every one has assured us they'll welcome you for dessert only. Even we are still amazed at the number of multi-star restaurateurs who are happy to accommodate you, though not necessarily at peak lunch and dinner hours. (And you may be seated at an elegant counter or more casual lounge area.) Simply let them know you've come just for dessert. The welcome will be as warm. The desserts are as good. The tab is a fraction of what a meal would cost.

As for the bakeries? The sheer number of them around the city has exploded, with more and more being started by young chefs leaving plum jobs in top establishments to set up shop on their own.

We envy you your discoveries.

adventure destinations

Ah, desserts. The ultimate comfort food. Our gastronomic equivalent of a cruise through the Greek islands or a summer weekend in the Hamptons. Pure pleasure. But wait! Something new is happening out there. Desert biking in Namibia. Subterranean rafting in New Zealand. And in the kitchens of New York's muscle-flexing young pastry chefs, desserts to challenge the most jaded palates, drawing upon the flavors of pungent cheeses, savory herbs, even vegetables like tomato, red pepper, and celery.

Nontraditional ingredients have been making guest appearances on dessert menus for years. Aquavit has featured a goat cheese parfait since the restaurant opened. Otto has been experimenting with gelati flavors like olive oil and goat cheese ricotta for years. You've been finding things like lavender crème brûlée and spice-accented chocolate sauces popping up all over town. Now a spirited band of young chefs are using sweet-salty-savory combinations excitingly to reshape entire dessert menus. Here are four to take your taste buds places they've never been before.

graffiti food and wine bar

✴ *224 East 10th Street at First Avenue*
  PHONE: 212-677-0695; 212-464-7743
  CREDIT CARDS: MC, V
  PRICE RANGE: $6
  WEB: www.graffitinyc.com

Jehangir Mehta's tiny East Village space has room for just eighteen diners at high tables, surrounded by Indian art interspersed with antiques from American shops and flea markets. The setting, entirely designed by Chef Mehta, is in line with his eclectic philosophy—both culinary and cultural. The name "Graffiti," refers, he says, to the writings of all cultures, a point he emphasizes with framed pages of Indian calligraphy and place mats of neatly folded international newspapers.

Children's brightly colored plastic chopsticks add a whimsical touch, but Graffiti's menu—eighteen mostly salty-sweet items—is sophisticated and imaginative. Only three items are exclusively "dessert," but two "borderline" dishes can be enjoyed as pre-dessert savories: a refreshing watermelon feta salad with mint sorbet, and tomato salad with balsamic olive sorbet. And, mmm, the desserts: the chocolate steamed bun with peanut butter ice cream, a warm-cold combo that turns the traditional Chinese bun into a deconstructed ice cream sandwich. (The warm chocolate filling flows out to meet the ice cream, more peanut-y than peanut buttery.) Halvah with mascarpone date cream (a revelation) with semolina substituting for the usual sesame, flecked with golden raisins and fresh green pistachios. An October visit found a seasonal special of mission figs, hot and juicy with a dollop of black-pepper ice cream. Along with Graffiti's uncommon desserts, look for extravagant cocktails like the pineapple grape tarragon salsa with peach tequila ice cream muddle (to be sipped or eaten with a spoon) and Prosecco Lychee Martini, an exquisite melding of fruit and sweet sparkling wines entirely new to our palates.

kyotofu

✣ *705 Ninth Avenue at 48th Street*

PHONE: 212-974-6012

CREDIT CARDS: AmEx, MC, V, Disc

PRICE RANGE: $7–15

WEB: www.kyotofu-nyc.com

The name tells you two things about Kyotofu: (1) It has a Japanese sensibility. (2) The menu is based largely on a single ingredient: tofu. Set in the hurly-burly heart of Hell's Kitchen, Kyotofu offers one of the city's most tranquil, refined, and appealing spaces. It is quite perfect for enjoying the amazing East-West fusion desserts being created by Ritsuko Yamaguci, last at the restaurant Daniel. Here, on her own, she's performing minor miracles with silken tofu, made fresh every day, in combination with flavorings not normally associated with Asian sweets—Tahitian vanilla, chocolate, nougat, maple, and mascarpone among them. The glassed-in kitchen up front gives you a chance to watch as chef Yamaguchi works her magic transforming basically bland tofu into toothsome wonders—puddings, pastries, ice creams and sorbets. The three-course kaiseki sampler provides an ideal introduction, offering perhaps the tofu cheesecake infused with pineapple and cherry purée, rich miso chocolate cake, and a Tahitian vanilla parfait made with maple soy mascarpone, toasted walnuts, and passion fruit caramel. During our visit, we spotted a young man spooning up what seemed to be purple pudding, which turned out to be black sesame sweet tofu with an unusual Jell-O-pudding texture, garnished with roasted green tea syrup, a white sesame tuile, and goji berries. Kyotufu has a wonderful selection of non-dairy tofu and soy-milk ice creams and sorbets (the yuzu-pineapple is outstanding) and an extensive sake and cocktail menu. You may opt for the fifteen-seat bar or the convex-walled back room, its white-tufted banquettes inducing the sensation of occupying a pristine Easter egg. All the baked goods are available for takeout. Kyotofu's tea sweets can also be found at TAKU New York in the Metropolitan Hotel, 569 Lexington Avenue at 51st Street.

p*ong

❊ *150 West 10th Street at Waverly Place*
PHONE: 212-929-0898
CREDIT CARDS: AmEx, MC, V, Disc
PRICE RANGE: $10–14; $15 minimum
WEB: www.p-ong.com

Pichet Ong, former pastry chef at Jean-Georges Vongerichten's 66 and Spice Market, brings his salty-sweet Asian sensibility to this intimate Village spot, where a unique three-part menu leads you from "savory" to "savory and sweet" to "sweet." Sit either at the bar or at one of P*ong's seven ash-wood tables to enjoy dishes that both surprise and tantalize. From the not-quite-dessert "sweet and savory" menu you might try the mini Stilton soufflé with a walnut crust and basil-arugula ice cream, a dish as pungently cheesy, nutty, and herbal as the name suggests. Equally unexpected—and perfect for summer—is Meyer lemon ice, with hints of salt, pepper, mint, and mascarpone. P*ong's "sweet" menu is a bracing departure from the sugar-shock induced by most conventional desserts: a tangy chevre cheese-cake daubed with pineapple and chocolate-coffee fudge, and a miso semifreddo—a sort of ice cream sandwich made with extra-virgin olive oil and sprinkled with crystallized wasabi and fresh strawberries. All the P*ong desserts have a carefully com-posed minimalist eye appeal, none more so than the delectable sesame-chocolate napoleon, a vision of lacy sesame-flavored chocolate layers piped with rich ricotta-orange ice cream, the whole drizzled with a ponzu caramel sauce and presented on a gold-woven place mat. Intriguing cocktails—from a chocolate mojito to a Blush, a mélange of sake, crème de mûre, vanilla, blackberries, and lychees—add to P*ong's exotic charms. For the more ascetic-minded, P*ong makes its own sodas in flavors like rhubarb and ginger, both delicious.

tailor

✳ *525 Broome Street bet. Thompson Street and Sixth Avenue*

PHONE: 212-334-5182

CREDIT CARDS: AmEx, MC, V, Disc

PRICE RANGE: sweet $11–$12; salty $16–17

WEB: www.tailornyc.com

The castle-like entrance to Tailor may suggest Dungeons & Dragons as much as haute dining. That's not altogether inappropriate. Tailor represents the invigorating edge in new-age cuisine; and the creations of co-owner/chef Sam Mason—his lauded stint as pastry chef at wd-50 behind him—can be both challenging and exciting. The menu is divided into just two sections of modest-sized dishes, "Sweet" and "Salty," but the line between the two is blurred, and you're encouraged to dance back and forth.

Of course, we went Sweet all the way. But Chef Mason isn't interested in flavors that have been tarted up to satisfy your conventional notions of what a chocolate sauce or cheesecake should taste like. In the latter, manchego cheese is used to provide a potent center, set atop the crunch of crushed graham crackers and almonds, accompanied by a piquant grape sorbet and a drizzle of fresh sage syrup. The unctuous black olive cake is draped with a robe of macerated blueberries and blueberry raisins, a pale yogurt sorbet cozying up to it. The spare menu listings only hint at the flavors packed onto each plate. Ask your knowledgeable server for more details. Or just follow your instincts and plunge in.

The dimly lit dining room is a multi-textured and -toned mix of turn-of-the-century preservation and postmodern industrial design. An old stairway takes you down to the casual skylight-domed bar area. Either space will happily serve you a little or a lot from the menu, and veteran bartender Eben Freeman's craftsman cocktails are fashioned with the same spirit of adventure. Root beer rye? House-smoked cola? Why not?

✳ new york's 50+ best

50+ best

(A to Z)

amai tea & bake house

❉ *171 Third Avenue bet. 16th and 17th Streets*
PHONE: 212-863-9630
CREDIT CARDS: AmEx, MC, V, Disc
PRICE RANGE: $.75–2.75; packaged cookies $10–38
WEB: www.amainyc.com

When Kelli Bernard moved to New York from California, she found she was cold all the time and turned to tea to warm up. As she developed a fascination with the many different blends, she began to use them in her baking, eventually selling her delicacies to Takashimaya and Ito En, where they are still available. Now she has turned her passion into a charming brick-walled tea and coffee bakery where *matcha*, the powdered green tea served traditionally in Japan, both flavors and tints many of the delicate baked goods, like the leaf-shaped chai-almond cookies that crumble like sugary air in the mouth, and the steamed red-bean muffin with smooth shiny dome that's a delicious foil for any type of tea beverage—green or smoky.

Kelli believes that chocolate and tea are great companions; green tea, for instance, washes the palette and complements the potent cacao bean. To this end, she also provides chewy brownies, some fruit-filled; cupcakes; and a fabulous truffle-y ball of chocolate mashed with dried fig. There's hot chocolate, too, one flavored with salty caramel. It comes with a floating cap of marshmallow—to keep it warm.

amy's bread

❉ *672 Ninth Avenue bet. 46th and 47th Streets*
PHONE: 212-977-2670
❉ *250 Bleecker Street at Leroy Street*

PHONE: 212-675-7802

CASH ONLY

PRICE RANGE: cake slices, bars, cookies, $2.25–4;
9-inch cakes, $35–40

WEB: www.amysbread.com

See also Chelsea Market page 35

Like the Energizer Bunny, Amy Scherber keeps baking, and baking, and baking. Her bread is justly famous, but her homey all-American desserts deserve accolades as well. The best selections are available in her Hell's Kitchen and West Village bakery cafés serving breakfast (scones, muffins, sticky buns, croissants) and lunch (fourteen sandwiches). For dessert (take-out, of course, if you wish) are six different kinds of layer cake, including old-fashioned yellow cake with chocolate icing, devil's food with chocolate silk icing, carrot cake with cream cheese frosting, coconut cake, and red velvet cake filled with butter cream. There are lemon bars too, and butterscotch cashew bars, brownies, and great big cookies that you'd expect to come out of a home kitchen—"kitchen sink"—dark-&-white chocolate, oatmeal, and coconut pecan. Amy says she uses slightly less sugar than many bakers to allow the real flavor of the ingredients—real butter and good chocolate—to come through. It does!

angelica kitchen

❋ *300 East 12th Street bet. First and
Second Avenues*

PHONE: 212-228-2909

CASH ONLY

PRICE RANGE: $4–5

WEB: www.angelicakitchen.com

Owner Leslie McEachern changes her dessert menu daily, but her loyal clientele doesn't seem to mind, whether it's pumpkin cheesecake (a mildly sweet and spicy wedge that we enjoyed on one visit), a chocolate mousse sundae with banana cream and almond praline, pistachio coconut tart, or any one of the great apple or spice cakes with maple tofu sauce and raspberry sauces. One of Angelica's most popular desserts is a fruit kanten parfait with nut cream, a gelled fruit dessert prepared using summer fruits or ripe pears. McEachern obtains as much of her produce as possible from local purveyors, not only fruits from organic farms in New York and Pennsylvania, but also sea vegetables from Maine, and maple syrup from northern Vermont. The glass-fronted restaurant is usually buzzing, and at dinner hour you can expect a wait for one of the rustic wooden tables. There's a large "family" table as well, for those seeking social interaction (although the management suggests that emotionally charged subjects should be avoided). No problem—think dessert.

balthazar

❋ *Spring Street bet. Broadway and Crosby Street*
PHONE: 212-965-1414
CREDIT CARDS: AmEx, MC, V
PRICE RANGE: $5.50–7.50
WEB: www.balthazarny.com

It was snowing outside the Spring Street windows the last time we stopped in at Balthazar—with no reservation—on a late winter afternoon. As we sank our forks through the yielding layers of caramelized bananas over a silken risotto cream on a crunchy butter crust, New York seemed roughly two thousand miles away.

Huge age-speckled mirrors on the walls. Long red-leather banquettes along the walls. Serpentine-topped glass-and-wood partitions to create intimate spaces. Terrazzo tiling underfoot and slowly revolving circular fans overhead. Every detail works in this wildly popular homage to the great fin-de-siècle Parisian brasseries.

The desserts are exactly what you want them to be: richly taste-and-textured recreations of the long-time staples of French bistro fare—a lightly brittle veneer atop an unctuous crème brûlée; an airy pavlova, its wispy meringue piled high with seasonal berries; profiteroles in a pool of good chocolate sauce; the freshest of buttery berry tarts.

Balthazar opens its doors at 7:30 a.m. and closes them after midnight on most days. Unless you love mobs and waits, pick an hour when *tout le monde* is unlikely to decide to join you there, and call ahead. It is an addictive experience.

balthazar boulangerie

✢ *80 Spring Street bet. Broadway and Crosby Street*
PHONE: 212-965-1785
CREDIT CARDS: AmEx, MC, V
PRICE RANGE: cake slices, $5; small tart, $5; large tart, $20

The turn-of-the-century décor and spirit of Balthazar spill over into the bakery, just next door. Its show-cases and display stands overflow with take-away treasures, facing a customer area that makes a rush-hour elevator seem like a wide open space. The struggle is worth it. All the Francophile temptations are there, and over to the left a blackboard announces the ever-changing seasonal specials. When we last looked, a lattice galette with orange marmalade-glazed pink rhubarb and bright red strawberries on puff pastry celebrated spring, along with Easter surprises like chocolate and hazelnut praline stuffed into genuine egg shells ($84 a dozen).

black hound

❖ *170 Second Avenue at 11th Street*
PHONE: 212-979-9505
CREDIT CARDS: AmEx, MC, V
PRICE RANGE: tarts, $1.50-5.50; pastries, $5-7.75; cakes, 3-inch, $5-7.75, 6-inch, $22.50-27.50
WEB: www.blackhoundny.com

Under a discreet black awning, Black Hound's window fairly pulsates with forbidden pleasures—chocolate cakes, nut cakes, cheese cakes, fruit pies, cream pies, fruit tarts, nut tarts, rum balls, mud balls, snow balls, cookies, candies, and confections. What's best? The busy bee chocolate cake is most popular (chocolate mousse, almond cake, marzipan, and almond liqueur), but we vote for the stunningly beautiful chocolate berry cup, a jumbo teacup made of chocolate and filled with almond cake, raspberry sauce, lemon curd, and whipped cream and bejeweled with glistening fresh fruits. It's irresistible as a special dessert to share with a friend or to bring as a gift when a knockout gift is called for. Given the complexity of many of Black Hound's desserts, they are surprisingly affordable.

blue smoke/jazz standard

✳ *116 East 27th Street at Lexington Avenue*

PHONE: 212-447-7733

CREDIT CARDS: AmEx, MC, V, Disc

PRICE RANGE: $7.25

WEB: www.bluesmoke.com

When it comes to desserts, expectations don't run high at Manhattan's BBQ joints—unless Danny Meyer, owner of Gramercy Tavern and Union Square Café, is at the helm. Down-home doesn't get any better 'round these parts than at his "urban barbecue," Blue Smoke. That doesn't mean that pastry chef Jennifer Giblin hasn't continued, like her predecessor, to temper things to suit New Yorkers' refined sensibilities. Could they be serving peach and blackberry cobbler with peach-buttermilk ice cream in Amarillo roadhouses? Are they flying in artisanal chocolate to mix with the Valrhona cocoa powder for the blowtorch-glazed frosting on a chocolate layer cake? (Ma'am, that is good!) Maybe signature desserts like their frozen strawberry cheesecake and Key lime pie have kissing cousins out there somewhere. We're not flying to Texas to find out. The atmosphere here is just-right casual. Ties are tolerated. Flying beer cans are not.

bouchon bakery café

✳ *10 Columbus Circle, 3rd level atrium*

PHONE: 212-823-9366

CREDIT CARDS: MC, V

PRICE RANGE: $7.75–8.50

Weather report: cloudy with a chance of brownies—not the ordinary kind, but dense, dark-chocolaty little numbers about the size and shape of champagne corks (*bouchon* means "cork" in French). It's a cool, misty afternoon, or it's sunny, or it's snowing—and you are at Bouchon Bakery, gazing east across Central Park South through Time Warner Center's immense glass facade. Whatever the weather, this restaurant guarantees two things: a magnificent New York view and a selection of outstanding desserts at one of celebrity chef Thomas Keller's multi-star eating establishments (the exclusive Per Se, with its nine-course, $250 tasting menu, is just upstairs; the legendary French Laundry is in Napa Valley). Happily, Bouchon Bakery is not only a (somewhat) price-friendly café offering classic bistro fare. It also boasts a stellar dessert menu designed by Sébastien Rouxel, executive pastry chef for all of the Keller restaurants. The signature chocolate bouchons are served two-to-a-plate usually with cherry ice cream, but on an August visit the bouchons arrived with a marvelously tangy ice cream made from the freshest apricots at the peak of ripeness. In presentation, the ice cream rested on a bed of pistachio crumbles alongside a peppery ribbon of juniper coulis. Next to this seductive mélange of flavors, the lemon meringue tart appeared like a pristine classic, its lemon curd filling rich and smooth in a buttery tart crust, the whole discreetly dribbled with a touch of caramel jam and citrus coulis. The Bouchon Bakery menu will always turn up seasonal surprises—blueberry lemon baba, for example, or tarte au poire, its flavors of wine-poached pear, almond streusel, almond milk sorbet, and chocolate pudding resonating like a string quartet in your mouth. And you can always depend on finding perennial favorites as well, like Pot de Crème, here described as a *cremeaux*, a mousse made with crème anglaisè exquisite in its cat-embossed white stoneware cup.

If you don't have time for a more formal sit-down tasting in the café, the retail bakery is just a few steps away. Here, the savory (soups, salads, sandwiches) and sweet offerings are lavish and available both for takeout and for consuming at high chairs and small tables. Along with most of the café's desserts, you'll find ribbon-wrapped packages of the must-have chocolate Bouchon brownies and buttery shortbreads, along with cookies, croissants, muffins, tea cakes, and all sorts of elegant patisserie items, including espresso éclairs and this town's most artfully designed fruit tarts. And (sound a high-pitched whistle) there are even treats for your dog, including, yes, foie gras dog biscuits ($2.50 each). Arf-ly good, or so we've heard.

brasserie 8 1/2

❊ *9 West 57th Street bet. Fifth and Sixth Avenues*
PHONE: 212-829-0812
CREDIT CARDS: AmEx, MC, V, Disc
PRICE RANGE: $8–25
WEB: www.rapatina.com/brasserie8

If NASA invents one of those infrared satellite imaging devices just for desserts, Brasserie 8 1/2 will show up as a hot spot. Dessert can be enjoyed here at any time, either in the stylish lounge area—walk down the winding staircase under a glowing vanilla-glass skylight—or in the spacious dining room; kids are welcome and the vibe is warm and inviting. All this and elegance too! Located at the hub of Manhattan's luxury marketplace—you're steps from Chanel, Bulgari, Vuitton, Tiffany's and more—this restaurant attracts a mixed crowd, from tourists to fashion editors often seen tapping at their laptops over lunch, as well as a pre-theatre contingent. Celebrity pastry chef Martin Howard—his alter ego, Choco-latina, is well-known to cooking-show viewers—has designed two spectacular dessert menus: Lounge Desserts are oversize confections meant for sharing; and single-serving desserts presented in three "acts"—seasonal sensations, signature sweets, and classic confections. Howard's down-home-with-a-twist approach to desserts is evident throughout, ranging from the Cupcake Quartet to milk chocolate cannolis. Can't decide? Go for the Grand Plateau, the totally-worth-it $25 selection of all the treats on the lounge menu—enough to get three or more people off to a start—beautifully presented on tiers of white chocolate. If the Plateau leaves you, amazingly, wanting more, Chef Howard's Frozen Banana Praline Soufflé—light, rich and not too sweet—is a good choice, as are Chocolate Poppers—bite-sized brioche filled with chocolate cream cheese (it works!) and served warm with butterscotch mousse (inspired by one of his mother's beloved recipes). Chocoholics can indulge their passion not just with the ubiquitous warm chocolate flourless cake, but with the brilliantly conceived Bento Box of Chocolates that includes cake, ice cream, an éclair, and a sweet sushi roll of rice pudding and roasted strawberries.

Sunday Brunch note: the restaurant offers two full buffets, one of which is entirely desserts and covers the lounge-area bar.

Wine with Your Dessert?

With pastry chefs like Martin Howard combining ingredients and flavors on a plate in ways that would have been unimaginable even a few years ago, wine stewards face the challenge of finding wines to match them, subtlety for subtlety. It's a challenge top wine stewards like Brasserie 8 1/2's Michel Boyer welcome. The selection is greater than ever; and, "I give the same attention to choosing the most sympathetic wine for each dessert," says Boyer. What to pair with the chef's special chocolate éclair, with its accents of coffee and vanilla? "A Bonny Doon Muscat from Santa Cruz."

If you're a novice and on your own, Boyer offers a few basics to guide you: champagnes for soufflés and ice creams, sauternes for cakes, ice wines for chocolate, and rosés for fruit tart. The pairings offered at more and more top restaurants like Brasserie 8 1/2 are a good, simple (and educational) way to get your bearings in this more rarified world of wine connoisseurship. Or put yourself into the hands of the sommelier, especially if everyone at table is ordering a different dessert. Just decide what your price limit is and say so. A good wine steward is pleased to know and even happier to find someone who's honest and interested.

bread bar

✳ *11 Madison Avenue at 25th Street*
PHONE: 212-889-0667
CREDIT CARDS: AmEx, MC, V
PRICE RANGE: Bread Bar, $6–8; Tabla, $8–9

A leisurely stroll through the area around Lexington Avenue and 27th and 28th Streets should turn up a pretty fair sampling of Indian pastries and sweets as they are served all over the city. Even a stop at Kalustyan, one of the city's most popular and well-stocked Indian groceries/delis/bakeries, is itself a culinary cultural education.

Leave it to Danny Meyer to take some of the basics—the spices, seeds, fruits, and flavors of India—and turn them into the unique cross-cultural cuisine at Bread Bar. We chose

Bread over the more elegant Tabla upstairs, because pastry chef Melissa Walknock's desserts for Bread stay a bit closer to their Indian roots; they're less formal, and more fun. Drop in any time after noon and you'll find Tahitian vanilla-bean kulfi, with warm ginger-peach compote. Even richer (if that's possible) is the dulce de leche Kulfi Pop, coated in dark chocolate and resting in a pool of caramel sauce. It makes the warm, featherweight doughnut holes, served with seasonal fruit compote, seem positively dietetic.

The room is a jumble of muted colors, natural materials, and eclectic styles—all very unintimidating.

tamarind tea room

❊ *43 East 22nd Street bet. Broadway and Park Avenue South*

PHONE: 212-674-7400

CREDIT CARDS: AmEx, MC, V

PRICE RANGE: $5

WEB: www.tamarinde22.com/tearoom.html

This modest appendage to the highly admired, upscale Indian restaurant Tamarind is the real thing, with a small selection of traditional Indian pastries, here made with a lighter, surer hand than New Yorkers are accustomed to. Each is accompanied on the menu by a recommended selection from the extensive tea offerings. Among the café desserts is *paysam*, a saffron-flavored vermicelli pudding with caramelized almonds. Creamlike in texture, it is rich-rich-rich. On request, you can also order dessert from the regular restaurant menu. We sampled the *ghujjia*, a light pastry stuffed with a lovely blend of semolina, raisins, coconut, and cashew nuts, with lemon sauce. The atmosphere is sleekly modern, with a few contemporary Indian prints for a cool touch of the east, and huge mirrors and windows to give the small space an expansive atmosphere.

lassi

❈ *28 Greenwich Avenue bet. 10th and Charles Streets*
PHONE: 212-675-2688
CREDIT CARDS: V, MC
PRICE RANGE: lassi yogurt drinks, $3.50–4.75; desserts, $4.50–10.50 (for two; or sauce on the side)
WEB: www.lassinyc.com

Heather Carlucci-Rodriguez is an up-and-comer. As pastry chef at L'Impero, she created many-splendored wonders rooted in Italy and Spain. Now she's got her own Lassi, an Indian street-food takeout shop with a different dessert every day. Pistachio-studded pumpkin Halwa pudding? Guava-mascarpone rice pudding? Whatever it is, we're betting it will be good. Lassi, the refreshing yogurt drink, is available here in flavors including lemon, cardamom, rose, mango, and "salty." That's good too.

bruno bakery

❈ *506 LaGuardia Place bet. Bleecker and Houston Streets*
PHONE: 212-982-5854

pasticceria bruno

: 1650 Hylan Blvd. in Staten Island

PHONE: 718-987-5859

WEB: www.pasticceriabruno.com

Award-winning chef Biagio Settepani took over at Bruno Bakery café and pasticceria in 1981, and has been turning out Italian pastry of consistently high quality ever since: freshly filled cannoli oozing with ricotta cream studded with chocolate chips and citron; *sfogliatelle* (crunchy clam-shaped layered pastries filled with ricotta and farina—best eaten warm); *zuppetta* (puff pastry layers filled with rum-flavored custard); and the so-called lobster tails, humongous crustacean-shaped shells filled with hazelnut cream. Chef Settepani provides French specialties as well, such as fruit tarts, chocolate mousse, crème brûlée, and mille-feuille; and with a nod to the Latin dessert trend, dulce de leche cheesecake with a milky caramel flavor. There are cookies, biscotti, sorbets, and gelatos and of course cannoli in classic Sicilian style—dipped in pistachio nuts on one end and candied orange peel on the other.

The Dolci Circuit

In the search for New York's best dolci, two East Village institutions, DeRobertis and Veniero's—just a cannoli's throw from each other—demand attention and respect. The product is comparable but the ambience differs mightily. **DeRobertis** (176 First Ave. at 11th St., 212-674-7137), founded in 1904 and still looking rather turn-of-the-twentieth-century, is a quiet tile-floored bakery with café tables in back that attract neighborhood people looking for a peaceful place to read the paper while enjoying espresso or cappuccino and, say, a piece of very good ricotta cheesecake or a *sfogliatella*. **Veniero's Pasticceria and Caffe** (342 E. 11th St. bet. First and Second Aves., 212-674-7070), established as a bakery around the same time, is more of a scene, with take-a-number lines at the front counter and café-goers filling the back area with lively conversation. The East Side Italian grocery store **Agata & Valentina** (1505 First Ave. at 79th St., 212-452-0690) sells moist ricotta cheesecake by the pound at their small espresso café, as well as other types of dolci worth exploring (shop during the week if possible to avoid the weekend crush and snaking checkout lines). Well worth a trip out to Brooklyn's Little Italy in Bensonhurst is **Villabate Pasticceria & Bakery** (7117 18th Ave. bet. 71st and 72nd Sts., 718-331-8430), which has gained the kudos of numerous New York baking kingpins and chefs who say the authentic confections are incomparable. In the Bronx, **Egidio Pastry Shop** (622 E. 187th St. at Hughes Ave., 718-295-6077) in the Arthur Avenue area is renowned for, you guessed it, cannoli!

café des artistes

* *1 West 67th Street bet. Columbus Avenue and Central Park West*

  PHONE: 212-877-3500

  CREDIT CARDS: AmEx, MC, V

  PRICE RANGE: $10–14

  WEB: www.cafenyc.com

Café des Artistes doesn't recreate a lost era in restaurant history. It's the real thing.

Howard Chandler Christy's famous murals of sparsely clad nymphs cavorting in flowery bowers were not started until 1934. But the artist had been one of the Hotel des Artistes' colorful tenants when the restaurant opened in 1917. Since then, the restaurant has welcomed everyone from Marcel Duchamp and Isadora Duncan to today's great stars of the nearby Metropolitan Opera—and now you, if you're feeling fin-de-siècle (and flush). The café's do-it-yourself fudge sundae has been retired, but the dark chocolate fondue for two has gleefully taken its place—a warm chocolate ganache with assorted fruits and cookies to delight the inner (or outer) child in anyone. A trio of crème brûlées—classic, lavender, and chocolate—is a lighter and neater alternative.

There is a small parlor bar off to one side of the lobby. But the place you want to be is the multilevel main restaurant, with its gaslight fixtures, deep colors, conservatory plants, and the murals. Pick an off-peak hour and tell them you're coming. They'll understand.

palm court at the plaza

❋ *768 Fifth Avenue at 59th Street*
PHONE: 212-759-3000
CREDIT CARDS: AmEx, MC, V
PRICE RANGE: $9.75

At least once in your life, you must experience New York's Gilded Age, as it survives in the Plaza's opulent Palm Court, now in its second splendidly refurbished incarnation. Sitting in its upholstered armchairs amid the soaring marble columns and palm trees, thick carpeting under your feet and a uniformed waiter hovering at your side, it's easy to imagine what life at the top must once have been like at least for an hour or two. You may make your selection from a table groaning under its platters of mousses, tortes, and Tatins. Such luxury comes at a price. Pay it. Remember, here money is no object.

café lalo

�֍ *201 W. 83rd Street at Amsterdam Avenue*
PHONE: 212-496-6031
CREDIT CARDS: AmEx, MC, V, Disc
PRICE RANGE: $1.25–6.50
WEB: www.cafelalo.com

West Siders have known of this dessert trove for years; for neighborhood newcomers, it's a revelation: more than one hundred kinds of cakes, pies, and tarts, including twenty-seven varieties of cheesecake. Then there are the cookies, pastries, rugelach, cannoli, biscotti, brownies, ice creams, zabaglione, frozen yogurt, fresh berries, and milkshakes! Cappuccino and espresso? Of course!

Styled as a Parisian café with floor-to-ceiling windows, it's so pretty that it's often selected as a location for commercials and movies, most notably *You've Got Mail* with Tom Hanks and Meg Ryan.

Brunch is served daily from 8 a.m. to 4 p.m., and the bar provides its evening crowd with a large selection of dessert wines, aperitifs, and other types of after-dinner drinks. Chocolate figures prominently in the offerings, with mousse cakes flavored with everything from Bailey's Irish Cream to passionfruit. The Viennese raspberry mousse cake is outstanding.

café sabarsky

❈ *1048 Fifth Avenue at 86th Street*
PHONE: 212-288-0665
CREDIT CARDS: AmEx, MC, V
PRICE RANGE: $7.50
WEB: www.cafesabarsky.com

Since opening in 2001, Café Sabarsky has established itself as such a fixture on the New York dining scene that it's hard to imagine a time when it wasn't here. Part of that comes from its setting, within the high-paneled library of the stately Miller-Vanderbilt mansion overlooking Central Park.

More important is the minute attention that chef-owner Kurt Gutenbruner has devoted to every detail in recreating the ambience and cuisine of its old-world Viennese counterparts. It shows in the precisely reproduced Wiener Werkstätte fixtures, the crisp white napery, the chairs, and china; all Austrian-made.

Finally, it all comes down to the food. And the desserts, each a classic, are as authentic and delicious as anything you'll find within Vienna's Ringstrasse: Sacher Torte, the most dark chocolate-robed cake with apricot confiture, just as it originated at Vienna's Hotel Sacher; Apfelstrudel, the café's bestseller, its pastry cocoon as tender as the succulent apples within; Topfentorte, a cheesecake that actually tastes of the farmer's cheese with which it's made, garnished with fresh berries. Everything, naturally, comes *mit schlag*, freshly whipped. Klimttorte, the ultra-rich medley of chocolate butter cream and hazelnut ganache, serves as a reminder that Café Sabarsky shares both the quarters and cultural heritage of the Neue Gallerie, the handsome museum founded by Serge Sabarsky and Ronald Lauder and devoted to the vibrant art of early twentieth-century Germany and Austria.

A hint: Café Sabarsky doesn't take reservations for lunch,

and you may face a wait. Go later, and consider ordering two desserts; at a bargain $7.50 each, you can indulge yourself. Note: Like the museum, closed Tuesdays.

wallsé

❉ *West 11th Street at Washington Street*

PHONE: 212-352-2300

CREDIT CARDS: AmEx, MC, V

PRICE RANGE: $11

WEB: www.wallse.com

Kurt Gutenbrunner has a second outpost of his Austro-Hungarian culinary empire on a quiet corner in the West Village. At Wallsé, open for dinner only, the emphasis is less on the classic Kaffeehaus desserts. Apple walnut strudel is a menu constant, as is the luscious Salzburger Nokerl, featherweight sweet dumplings showered with huckleberry sauce. If Mohr im Hemd is on the menu, that's the chocoholic's dessert of choice, a chocolate hazelnut soufflé-like cake served warm from the oven.

carrot top

❉ *3931 Broadway bet. 164th and 165th Streets*

PHONE: 212-927-4800

❉ *5025 Broadway bet. 213th and 214th Streets (the original twenty-three-year-old location)*

PHONE: 212-569-1532

CREDIT CARDS: AmEx, MC, V, Disc

PRICE RANGE: cookies, $.50–2.50; cakes and slices, $5–6

ATTENTION: All Customers Illegally Parked.
Please give us your orders, we will bring it to your car.
Traffic officers will give you a ticket!!

So reads the sign over the counter of this longtime and well-loved bakery café in Washington Heights. It's the kind of place where everybody knows your name—or greets and treats you as though they did.

The name is the giveaway to what Carrot Top does best: carrot cake, speckled with nuts and spices, moist, scrumptious, and available whichever way you like it: a square slab, two layers, three layers, or "special," each slathered with old-fashioned whipped cream cheese frosting. There's even a CD-sized carrot cookie (which is, basically, spread-out carrot cake). We broke open a carrot muffin late one morning right from the oven, a steamy cloud rising from its center.

There are all kinds of pies (including sweet potato, cherry crumb, and at holiday time, pecan) and cakes (Black Forest is now the best-seller), all made from recipes passed down from owner Renée Mancino's grandmother, and now on to Renée's daughter, Nikki.

Do your sampling in the functional main room or the slightly fancier green room off to the side. Or place your order and run for the car.

It's all the same at Carrot Top's original, twenty-three-year-old location.

~~~~~~

ceci-cela patisserie

❖ *55 Spring Street bet. Lafayette and Mulberry Streets*
PHONE: 212-274-9179
CREDIT CARDS: MC, V

166 Chambers Street bet. Broadway and
Greenwich Street
PHONE: 212-566-8933
CREDIT CARDS: AmEx, MC, V
WEB: www.ceci-celapatisserie.com
PRICE RANGE: pastries, $3.75–4; individual cakes, $6;
mini pastries $.50–1

Opened in 1992, Ceci-Cela is the kind of place that seems to have been there forever and makes you wish you lived upstairs and could easily pop down for a perfect pain au chocolat every morning, and a piece of quiche at lunchtime (there's a tiny exposed-brick back room with a few tables) and any one of their truly wonderful pastries or cakes for dessert every night. The large talents behind the little space (two people can barely pass each other between the wall and the pastry case) are French chefs Laurent Dupal and Hervé Grall, both veterans of legendary restaurants owned by Drew Nieporent.

Best-sellers, and justly so, are the raspberry-and-blueberry tart and the light and lovely raspberry chocolate mousse cake; but the selections will test your resistance to such Gallic delicacies as the napoleon with fresh raspberries, and the crème brûlée with bergamot flavor. Dupal and Grall and Chef Gerard Fioravanti welcome special orders for personalized cakes; and when you're wondering what enchanting gift to bring to an exacting foodie friend, look no further than Ceci-Cela's Fancy Petit Fours Box of a dozen exquisite miniatures for $25.

cendrillon

❊ *45 Mercer Street bet. Broome and Grand Streets*
PHONE: 212-343-9012
CREDIT CARDS: AmEx, MC, V, Disc
PRICE RANGE: $6.50–8
WEB: www.cendrillon.com

Once upon a time, Soho was the place to go for the fresh, the unexpected, the stimulating, the exciting. At Cendrillon, it still is.

Here, behind a modest facade on the southernmost reaches of Mercer Street, one of New York's most adventuresome chefs continues to blur the lines between Eastern and Western cuisines. He's Romy Dorotan, and he brings the principles and techniques of the French cooking in which he was trained to the cuisine of his native Philippines. His success comes from not only his talent but also from his zeal in introducing an A-list of Philippine ingredients virtually unknown in the United States. Cassava bibingka with mangosteen-palm-sugar ice cream is not something you improvise from the Union Square greenmarket.

What should you try? We loved the mango tart—Romy's version of the traditional tarte Tatin—its paper-thin, crunchy, torched crust resting on top of a distinctively spiced sweet mango base. Buko pie—*buko* being young, unripened coconut—came with a fruity, barely sweet rhubarb sauce when we had it (accompanied by the chef's own vanilla-bean ice cream). Buko sorbet accompanies a blueberry-and-purple-yam tart. Kalamansi meringue pie is made from a mild variety of lime Romy brings in from the Philippines.

Ever the experimenter, Romy has lately been exploring the exotic potential of U.S.-grown ingredients. Avocados, watermelon, and smoked maple syrup—a rare commodity from Vermont—have inspired luscious new ice cream and sorbet flavors, and red-fleshed Massachusetts apples have found their way into a tangy-sweet seasonal tart that glows like molten rubies.

Everyone from Alice Waters to Cindy Sherman has dropped by Cendrillon's low-key, sophisticated space to sample the exotic and modestly priced dinner menu. Dessert is the perfect start.

chelsea market

❋ *75 Ninth Avenue bet. 15th and 16th Streets*
PHONE: 212-255-7990
WEB: www.chelseamarket.com

Cookies, brownies, cakes, pies, ice cream, and more—it's all here at the booming block-deep, 800-foot long market, where many of our favorite bakeries have expanded their retail operations, making room for more great desserts. Note: Most establishments close at 7 p.m. during the week and 6 p.m. on weekends. (Take a nine-minute podcast tour of the market at: www.dailyvodcasts.com.)

Eleni's New York (212-255-7990; www.elenis.com) now has a 30-foot-long cupcake and cookie bar where fancifully hand-iced cookies (her designs or yours) are optimally displayed. Look for soft-baked sugar cookies, such as snickerdoodles, chocolate chip, and oatmeal raisin; and heart-shaped "love" brownies (also available at Dean & DeLuca, Grace's Marketplace, Bergdorf Goodman, Neiman Marcus, Citarella, Macy's, and Saks). Price range: cupcakes $2–3; regular cookies, $.60–1.25; designer cookies, $1.00 each. At **Fat Witch Bakery** (212-807-1335, www.fatwitch.com), look for eight varieties of Patricia Helding's cutely packaged brownies, including the basic No-Nut brownie, fudgey and perfect; Red Witch, chock-full of luscious dried cherries; Walnut, the basic model plus crunch; and Java, chocolate with a coffee jolt. The shop also sells gift boxes and ships almost anywhere. Price range: $1.25–2.50. This outpost of **Sarabeth's Bakery** (212-989-2424, www.sarabeth.com) has a sampling of the baked goods served at the shop's other locations (see Index): sour cream, buttermilk, and cream-cheese cakes, Bundt cakes, loaf cakes, cookies, and cupcakes. Chocolate favorites include a light chocolate soufflé cake and a rich and famous chocolate truffle cake. Price range per slice: about $4. Although **Amy's Bread** (212-462-4338, www.amysbread.com) has its main bread-baking operation here, the selection of her homey, American-style desserts is more complete at the other two locations (see page 14). **Ruthy's Bakery & Café** (212-463-8800) specializes in rugelach in eight flavors (we like apricot and raspberry) but her old-fashioned carrot cake is fine too, as is the New York-style cheesecake. There are ready-made special-occasion cakes; or place an order for any shape or design, from Pooh to a graduate's mortarboard. Price range: cookies and rugelach, $11.95/lb; cakes per slice, $3.95–4.95; whole cakes, $14.95–49.95. **Ronnybrook Milk Bar** (212-741-6455, www.ronnybrook.com) offers breakfast, lunch, and an expanded milk-based menu. Deliciously rich organic ice creams are available by pint, scoop, or bowl (including ice cream in a doughnut bowl and hot fudge sundaes with the works at $4–4.75); as well as ice cream cookie sandwiches ($3), combo shakes ($4.75–5) and blended milk and yogurt "cocktails" ($4.25). Cups or cones: small $1.75 (kids), $2.71

(single), $3.52 (double); pints $4.25 (unusual flavors include cinnamon, cardamon ginger crème brûlée, and pumpkin). The tiny gelateria, **Gelato dei Presidi** (www. meno18.com), tucked just to the right of the cavernous emporium Buon Italia, has wonderful flavors made from Italian and Sicilian ingredients. Don't miss it! End your stroll through the market at **T Salon** (212-243-0432; www.tsalon.com), where you can enjoy a civilized sit-down with tea and cakes, or take out one of their moist fruit brownies ($4) or fancy desserts (crêpe cake; triple mousse cake, $8 each).

chikalicious

✳ *203 East 10th Street bet. First and Second Avenues*
PHONE: 212-995-9511
CREDIT CARDS: AmEx, MC, V
PRICE RANGE: Prix Fixe, $12 (amuse, choice of dessert and petit fours; with wine paring add $7); wines, ports, sherries, and cocktails $8–13 per glass, $22–92 by the bottle; coffee and tea $3–3.50. No reservations accepted.
WEB: www.chikalicious.com

No entrees. No tapas. No salty. No savory. ChikaLicious was the first New York restaurant to go all sweets. So its energies are channeled into nothing but transforming old dessert favorites into new extravaganzas. Like, say, a chocolate tart with pink peppercorn ice cream and red-wine sauce, or lemon-verbena panna cotta with cantaloupe sorbet and toasted pistachios, or white chocolate mousse and almond tuile napoleon with a marvelously pungent concord grape sorbet and a gelée of Brachetto d'aqui Coppo 2003 (an Italian dessert wine). Brilliantly conceived and beautifully plated desserts such as these are served up in a tiny modernist space, where co-owner Chika Tillman and assistants work their confectionary magic. Sit at the ten-seat counter for an optimal view of the chefs as they shape, dip, and arrange their precious homemade ingredients on lovely china plates. The very popular Fromage Blanc Island cheesecake, for example, is presented floating atop a sea of crushed ice. Your order is preceded by an *amuse* of the day—it might be a smoky Darjeeling tea gelée with an ovoid dollop of cinnamon sorbet served in a tiny white porcelain dish. After your sweet "main course" (paired, if you wish, with wines, coffees, or teas), a plate of tiny petit fours materializes to be popped in the mouth accompanied by oohs and aahs—a tiny cube of coconut-coated marshmallow, perhaps, or an intense, marble-sized chocolate truffle perfumed with mint and lemon. ChikaLicious caters to the after-dinner crowd—there's often a wait—staying open Wednesday through Sunday from 3 p.m. to 11:30 p.m. The high-concept menu changes seasonally, however, so be prepared for surprises.

Note: As we went to press, ChikaLicious Puddin' mainly takeout—opened nearby (204 East 10th Street; 212-475-0929) with a never-changing 3-item menu: apple pudding with custard sauce; brioche bread pudding with custard sauce; and chocolate.

chocolate destinations

You know that craving you get when it seems as though only chocolate will do? There's hardly a destination in this book that doesn't make sure you'll find something deeply indulgent to satisfy it. A few go all the way and devote themselves wholeheartedly to this most passionate of sweet addictions.

One of the most celebrated names in chocolate, Michel Cluizel reinvented his New York shop in 2007 as **Dessert Studio at Chocolat Michel Cluizel** (ABC Carpet and Home, 888 Broadway at 19th St., 212-477-7335; www.chocolatmichelcluizel-na.com), serving not only its incomparable truffles, bonbons, and hot chocolate (shots or cups), but also the celebrated pastries, ice creams, and sorbets of Will Goldfarb, along with Seth Greenberg's exquisite little chocolate chip cookies and brownies. Add to that lineup Terzi coffee (also available for takeout at $40 a pound), fine wines, and chocolate-spiked cocktails, all to be savored at one of six rustic tables or a sleek curving glass bar. Weekly chocolate and chocolate-spirit tastings are available by appointment at $35–$100 per person.

For more haute French chocolate bliss, head up to the cocoa-colored tea rooms of **La Maison du Chocolat** (30 Rockefeller Plaza at 49th St., 212-265-9004, 1018 Madison Ave. bet. 78th and 79th Sts., 212-744-7117, www.lamaisonduchocolat.com/en), where you can find hand-dipped chocolates, tea cakes, tarts, and cookies including florentines and macaroons in five chocolate flavors. (Hint: try the Andalousie—almond-chocolate biscuit, bitter chocolate truffle mousse, and fresh lemon cream. *Incroyable!*) May through September add to the list sorbets and ice creams like caramel and candied chestnut; for the holidays, an individual Bûche de Noël.

The Madison Avenue location holds tastings Thursdays and Saturdays, reservations required.

The complete chocoholic will have **The Chocolate Room** (86 Fifth Ave. bet. St. Mark's Place and Warren St., in Brooklyn, 718-783-2900, www.the chocolateroombrooklyn.com) on speed dial. In a romantic French setting, you face choosing among black bottom butterscotch custard, the brownie sundae, a three-layer blackout cake (Oprah's choice, if you're asking), and the ultimate fondue for two of 60 percent Belgian chocolate with pound cake, fresh fruit, and homemade marshmallows for dipping.

Connoisseurs of hot chocolate have long flocked to **MarieBelle's Cacao Bar** (484 Broome St. bet. Wooster St. and West Broadway, 212-925-6999; 762 Madison Ave. bet. 65 and 66th Sts., 212-249-4585, www.mariebelle.com/cafe.cfm), where five house-specialties include a justly-famous Euro-style Aztec hot chocolate made from single-origin cacao beans, along with mocha and spiced varieties. Enjoy a cup with a pastry or the sinful excess of molten chocolate cake.

Hot chocolate flows sweet and—if you wish—spicy every day at **Jacques Torres Chocolates** (350 Hudson St. at King St.; 285 Amsterdam Avenue at 73rd St., both in Manhattan; 66 Water St. at Plymouth St., Brooklyn; all locations: 212-414-2462; www.mrchocolate.com), among the best in any borough, as are the flaky croissants and pains au chocolat served up every morning. On Saturdays only, the former pastry chef-turned master chocolatier returns to his roots, making a *pithivier*, or fruit tart, or a crinkly-layered napoleon so good it will have you licking the paper—whatever strikes your fancy. At Torres's Hudson Street location, a big glass wall allows you to watch the chocolate-making process in action, a guaranteed kid-pleaser, especially with a big chocolate cookie or brownie in hand. Torres, by now a New York institution, happily provides dozens of sweet ways to take him home with you, from champagne truffles to chocolate-covered you-name-its.

Annual Chocolate Events

Winter in New York means full chocolate immersion.

November: The Chocolate Show! Don't miss this fabulous, three-day event with tastings, culinary demonstrations, and products by sixty-five top chocolate makers. Renowned chefs and chocolatiers demonstrate their art; there are book signings, educational exhibits, and children's activities too. The Place: The Metropolitan Pavilion, 125 West 18th Street, bet. Sixth and Seventh Aves. For info: 212-889-5113. Tickets: 866-CHOCNYC; online at www.chocolateshow.com (for dates and programs as well); www.ticketmaster.com, or 212-307-7171. Adults $28; children under 5 free; children 5–12 free, with two-child limit per adult.

February: It might be snowing but love and chocolate are in the air. The Ritz-Carlton's 14th floor Rise bar, with breathtaking views of New York harbor, is the romantic setting for a sumptuous chocolate buffet—twenty dessert selections by pastry chef Laurent Richard and a bottomless glass of champagne—offered throughout the month on Friday and Saturday nights, including Valentine's Day, of course! (Battery Park City, 2 West St. For prix fixe information and reservations 6:30, 8:30, or 10:30 seatings call 212-344-0800.)

Chocolate Tours

For chocoholics, it's the ultimate mini vacation—several hours spent exploring New York's finest chocolatiers with an expert guide.

Chocolate Tours of NYC (www.chocolatetoursnyc. com) arranges customized half- or full-day walking itineraries for groups of six or more through Soho, the West Village, Union Square, and the Upper East Side. With multilingual culinary historian Alexandra Leaf as your guide, you'll learn how chocolate is made, enjoy tastings at every stop, and become savvy about trends in the world of chocolate. Prices start at $65 per person; participants must be 18 or older; reservations: 646-637-8100 or through the website.

Chocolate Zoom magazine sponsors New York Chocolate Tours (www.sweetwalks.com) with a choice of either "luxury" (Upper East Side) or "new cuisine" (Soho) itineraries for about $70 per person; for reservations call 917-292-0680.

city bakery

❋ *3 West 18th Street bet. Fifth and Sixth Avenues*
PHONE: 212-366-1414
CREDIT CARDS: AmEx, V, MC
PRICE RANGE: cookies, $2–3; tarts, $5
WEB: www.thecitybakery.com

You don't have to ask many savvy New Yorkers where they go for brownies, lemon tarts, and chocolate chip cookies before you'll hear the name City Bakery.

Ilene Rosen is the chef who carries off this feat on a daily basis. The brownie? It fits most brownie-lovers' idea of nirvana: thick, dense, chewy, and *echt*-chocolatey. The lemon tart is the subtlest balance of sweet and sour in a just-right light custard that is melty and zingy on the tongue. Among the seasonal fruit tarts, a fall special has cranberries that burst with flavor under an avalanche of brightly caramelized slivered almonds. The melted chocolate cookie is everything the name implies, and should only be ordered if your desire for chocolate recognizes absolutely no boundaries. Even the marshmallows are a homemade glory.

The hum of contented New Yorkers provides most of the atmosphere in this high-ceilinged, industrial-spare Flatiron spot, with cafeteria-style service and seating. Lunchtime is prime time at City Bakery, with a full-tilt takeout crowd vying at the cash registers with tray-toting moms who park their strollers alongside the banquettes. Things quiet down late afternoon through the dinner hour, affording sweets-seekers quietude in which to savor their own favorite sugar fixes.

birdbath

❋ *223 First Avenue near 13th Street*
PHONE: 646-722-6565
CASH ONLY

✳ *145 Seventh Avenue South at Charles Street*
PHONE: 646-722-6570
PRICE RANGE: cookies, $2.50; muffins, $2.50–3
CREDIT CARDS: AmEx, MC, V
WEB: www.buildagreenbakery.com

City Bakery's whimsically named "green" offshoot features many of the same luscious cookies, brownies, tarts, and muffins available at the mother ship. But the point seems to be the shop itself, which is made—floors, counters and walls—from sustainable, even edible, materials. But please don't chew the scenery; these shops are small enough.

cones: ice cream artisans

✳ *272 Bleecker Street bet. Jones and Morton Streets*
PHONE: 212-414-1795
CASH ONLY
PRICE RANGE: cones, $3.75; pints, $9.50–18; cakes, $28, $38, $50

Brothers Raul and Oscar D'Aloisio call what they sell ice cream, but it has a rich gelato-like texture similar, they say, to the confection they grew up with as members of the large Italian community in Argentina. They opened Cones in 1998, creating "straight" flavors. "We don't do Chunky Monkey," says Raul. Indeed, Cones's flavors, like strawberry, mango, and canteloupe, are deceptively simple, but pure and rich, as are the outstanding "special flavors" like the best-selling dulce de leche, rum-laced tiramisu, Marsala-tinged zabaglione, and white chocolate. In 1999 Eric Asimov of the *New York Times* called Cones "some of the best ice cream in the city—rich, smooth, and deeply enough flavored to reawaken taste buds that have forgotten how good ice cream can be." Every year, for a few weeks at the height of the summer, Cones offers the extraordinary Lemon D.P., a reduction of Dom Perignon champagne mixed with lemon sorbet that sells for $18 a pint. Cones also takes special orders for ice cream cakes which the brothers make up on the spot from that day's freshly made ice cream. Cones typically has lines out the door and down the block. Still, says Raul, "New York is not really an ice cream city. In Argentina, there's a gelateria on every block and people are willing to pay more for a good product. Here you have to sell a lot of cones to pay the rent." On our visit, the store was packed and it seemed that New Yorkers were doing their bit, consuming large quantities of the brothers' delectable product, as sort of an ongoing rent party.

Ice cream? Gelato? What's the dif'?

Here's how the subject of quiescent desserts breaks down, with thanks to *Food Lover's Companion* by Sharon Tyler Herbst.

Ice Cream: The dairy product we know and love is made from cream and other milk products, such as condensed and dry milk. To this is added sugar or other sweeteners—in some cases honey or corn syrup or artificial sweeteners. Finally, solids are tossed in—chocolate chunks, nuts, fruit, and so forth. The FDA stipulates that ice creams with "solid additions" have at least 8 percent milk fat; 10 percent for plain ice creams. Ice cream also necessarily contains air—termed "overrun" by the FDA—to give it a soft, scoopable texture. Commercial ice creams may have overrun of between

20 to 50 percent, and may include emulsifiers, stabilizers, and artificial flavors, among other additions. The home-made ice creams served in many fine restaurants are free of additives.

Ice Milk: Basically ice cream with less milk fat and milk solids.

Gelato: Italian ice cream (the word literally means "iced" in Italian). Gelato contains less air and therefore has a denser, creamier texture than American ice cream. Egg yolk is sometimes used in gelato, but most often it's a milk/cream-based product.

Gelateria: A shop or café where gelato is sold.

Sorbet: The French word for a frozen, water-based confection that never contains milk and is usually made with fruit and fruit juices or other flavorings. The Italians call it *sorbetto*, which comes from the verb *sorbire*, meaning to "slush it up," appropriate to its lovely texture.

Sherbet: The same as sorbet, but a variation may contain milk, egg whites, and/or gelatin. The word is derived from the Arabic *sharbet* or *charbet*, a cold drink of sweetened fruit juice. The Arabs are said to have learned about cold or frozen desserts from the Chinese, who first thought of adding sweet flavorings to snow.

French Ice Cream: Ice cream with a base of egg custard.

Frozen Custard: Genuine frozen custard differs from ice cream in that it contains at least 1.4 percent egg yolk. Like ice cream, it contains at least 10 percent milk fat, although many custards today are low-fat. The best frozen custard is made in a "continuous flow" machine that does not beat air into the mixture.

Granité, Granita: see Ice.

Ice: An ice (as in lemon ice), is a water-based frozen confection with a relatively low sugar content and a more granular texture than sorbet.

craft

❈ *43 East 19th Street bet. Broadway and Park Avenue South*
PHONE: 212-780-0880
CREDIT CARDS: AmEx, MC, V
PRICE RANGE: pastries, $8; ice creams and sorbet, $4
WEB: www.craftrestaurant.com

When Craft opened, it famously discovered that its create-your-own dishes concept was a little too high for most people, and it settled into a more braised-or-grilled norm. Its dessert menu matches the main menu in its reliance on the highest quality in-season ingredients, fresh daily from the Greenmarket and select near-city farms. But all the choices are made by pastry chef Karen DeMasco.

This is someone you can trust. Always among her daily choices, we're promised, will be the extraordinary Brioche Pain Perdu, ("like the best French toast you've ever tasted," as one guest described it) airy with a hint of sweetness, enhanced by sautéed apples and a generous dollop of caramel ice cream. Cinnamon sugar doughnuts are also among the unexpected offerings to find their way to first-class menus. Craft's are feathery light and filled with multiple flavors, with sauces for dipping.

On one visit, olive oil cake with caramelized apples and olive oil sabayon was on the menu, as was a single-slice pineapple upside-down cake, just as buttery and sweet as our fondest memories.

If the restaurant's name stirs thoughts in your head of the Arts and Crafts movement, they're reinforced by the handsome dark woods set against the high beige-toned walls. Think restful—especially at lunch, when the lack of high-rise-office conferencers keeps the decibel level low.

craftbar

✳ *900 Broadway bet. 19th and 20th Streets*
PHONE: 212-461-4300
CREDIT CARDS: AmEx, MC, V, Disc
PRICE RANGE: $9

Now in a new location, Craftbar remains a charmingly informal space—cool and dark—with a less-pricey menu that includes desserts by Craft's Karen DeMasco that can be ordered anytime, from noon to midnight. An apple fritter and caramel ice cream combo is almost always on the menu by popular demand. Her puddings are silken delights, and the brown-sugar cake with roasted pineapple and vanilla ice cream is a perfect medley of flavors and textures.

craftsteak

✳ *85 10th Avenue at 15th Street*
PHONE: 212-400-6699
CREDIT CARDS: AmEx, MC, V, Disc
PRICE RANGE: $6–12

As a recent addition to restaurateur Tom Colicchio's

Crafty-empire, Craftsteak—located in the trendy meatpacking district—has gotten a lot of buzz. But you can forget all that and just relax in the spacious lounge (any time after 6 p.m., and at a table with a Hudson River view if you're lucky), marveling over the specialties of pastry chef Erica Leahy. The most special: PIES!—virtually unknown in New York haute dessertery circles, it seems— here baked in a delicate buttermilk crust with seasonal fillings (strawberry/rhubarb and Meyer lemon meringue are two) and served á la mode. If you're very, very lucky the chocolate hazelnut tart, with a crunchy shortbread crust, chewy poached apricots, hazelnut brittle, and caramel ice cream will be on the menu as well. The homemade ice creams and sorbets—served as three- or six-scoop samplers—are particularly good, with concord grape, fennel, ginger, and caramel topping our list.

'wichcraft

See website for locations: www.wichcraftnyc.com
CREDIT CARDS: AmEx, MC, V
PRICE RANGE: $1.50-2

Craft's proliferating eat-in/take-out sandwich bars have terrific breakfast and lunch sandwiches and panini ($5–9), but the ice cream sandwiches are not to be missed—try banana ice cream between oatmeal cookies—nor are the brownies, lemon bars, and 'wich cookies in chocolate cream and peanut butter versions.

daniel

❉ *60 East 65th Street bet. Madison and*
Park Avenues
PHONE: 212-288-0033
CREDIT CARDS: AmEx, MC, V, Disc
PRICE RANGE: $16
WEB: www.danielnyc.com

new york's 50+ best places to enjoy dessert

"So beautiful!" That will be your reaction the first time you step through Daniel's famous doors. Housed and decorated in palatial neo-Renaissance style, Daniel is haute in every sense of the word, reaching its pinnacle, appropriately, in the flawlessly prepared, innovative French-inspired cuisine of celebrated chef-owner Daniel Boulud. It may seem incredible that you can indulge in one of pastry chef Eric Bertoia's ravishing desserts, in so sumptuous a setting, for—what?—under $25 a person, including coffee and tip. Among recent arrivals on the constantly changing seasonal menu: banana-manjari chocolate clafouti with macadamia nougat and caramel ice cream; mango and raspberry vacherin with ginger ice cream. The dark chocolate caramel bombe with passionfruit cream is the enduring classic. "So, where did you go last night?" "Daniel, and we had such a wonderful time." You bet!

david burke & donatella

❉ *133 East 61st Street bet. Park and*
Lexington Avenues
PHONE: 212-813-2121
CREDIT CARDS: AmEx MC, V
PRICE RANGE: $10–18
WEB: www.dbdrestaurant.com

Trellises and cushy white leather bar-chairs set a bright suburban tone as you enter this ultra-fashionable restaurant, where Chef David Burke has established a reputation for trendy, innovative food—served with theatrical flourishes. A table by the front window next to the bar is the perfect place to enjoy a mid-afternoon treat of several of Burke's signature desserts. The runaway bestseller is the Cheesecake Lollipop Tree, a holiday-like silver tree atremble with ten lollipops ornamentally inserted, some dipped in three kinds of chocolate and nuts, some in Heath bar crunch, and some two-fruit flavored. The tasty two-bite pops (which Burke has patented) come with a side of bubble gum-flavored whipped cream (or for anyone not a bubble-gum fanatic, plain). But there's more to Burke than pops, notably the oft-praised butterscotch panna cotta, served in a martini glass with swirls of curried chocolate sauce and honey gelée and topped with sticks of curried meringue for dunking. And yes, the curry-spiced butterscotch spins deliciously in your mouth, with chocolate as the anchor. In another winner, Chocolate^3, pastry chef Gustavo Tzoc plays the chocolate card to the max with a plated three-part confection: a chocolate-almond-cherry tart, a rich cream, and a dollop of cocoa nib ice cream, complete with toasted chopped cocoa beans and caramel crumbles. Chef Tzoc brings his Guatemalan heritage to bear on a simple-sounding but deceptively complex and delicious coconut layer cake that turned out to be delightful mélange of tropical flavors. Coconut anglaisé fills the biscuit-y layers and ices the cake, which comes with a puddle of passion-fruit sauce and a squiggle of strawberry consommé. Other winners: the homey caramelized warm apple tart, served with a nicely tangy cider caramel; the chocolate caramel mousse, served on a block of salt sprinkled with peanuts; and then there's Mango the Hedgehog, a toy-like critter with multicolored meringue "quills" on a dome of mango and raspberry puree and served with a raspberry creamsicle and a gold-leaf chip on a fresh berry. Remember, we did say "theatrical."

david burke @ bloomingdale's

✻ *1000 Third Avenue, entrance on 59th Street bet. Lexington and Third Avenues*
PHONE: 212-705-3800
CREDIT CARDS: AmEx, MC, V, Disc
PRICE RANGE: desserts, $8.95; Burke in the Box takeout, $1.25–3.95
WEB: www.burkeinthebox.com,
www.davidburke.com/bloomingdales

As you enter on 59th Street, the full-service restaurant Burke Bar Café is at left, the takeout shop, Burke in the Box, to the right. The café offers breakfast, lunch, and a dinner-cum-wine bar at night. A full dessert menu is offered that might include spumoni panna cotta, carrot cake, or a s'more sundae. As with any major restaurant, go off-peak, between lunch and dinner, or late night, if you plan to go just for dessert.

Burke in the Box offers, in addition to soups, salads and other savories, cheesecake lollipops ($1.45 per pop, 3 for $3.95); mini cupcakes, jello, and puddings.

edgar's café

✻ *255 West 84th Street bet. Broadway and West End Avenue*
PHONE: 212-496-6126
CASH ONLY
PRICE RANGE: cake slices and tiramisu, $5.25; pies, $4.95; gelato and sorbetto, $5.25

If it's true that Edgar Allen Poe completed "The Raven" in a house on this stretch of Manhattan's West Side (renamed Edgar Allen Poe Street between Broadway and Riverside Drive), we can only hope that the famously melancholy poet had as cozy a café to write in as this namesake haunt favored by New York artists, writers, and theater people.

The owners have designed it as a faux-bohemian hangout, complete with trompe-l'oeil crumbling stucco walls, old tile and slate floor, marble-topped tables, and café chairs with wrought iron backs. Fans of Edgar's know it as one of the city's great dessert destinations, with more than eighty different cakes (at least twelve chocolate varieties), pies, tarts, and other confections—many of them kosher—available at all times along with espresso and cappuccino. A portion of the cakes, such as the berry-laden, sugar-sprinkled Frutti di Bosco tart, are imported from Bindi of Milan. Among the chocolate selections are locally made rich mousse cakes, and the popular chocolate mud and Black Forest cakes. And the tiramisu? Made on premises, this ultra-creamy melange of ladyfingers, espresso, mascarpone, and chocolate is a perfect balance of flavors and textures that, as a bonus, packs a potent rum-kahlua punch. It's simply one of the best we've had in New York.

Weekdays it's a quiet place to read the paper or work at your laptop. Weekends, Edgar's fills up with a brunch crowd ordering French toast, Belgian waffles, and fruit-topped Greek yogurt and rugelach, sugar-free if you like. And at all times, there are snacks and sandwiches that kids love.

eileen's special cheesecake

* *17 Cleveland Place, corner of Kenmare and Centre Streets opposite Lafayette and Spring Streets*

PHONE: 212-966-5585

CREDIT CARDS: AmEx, MC, V, Disc

PRICE RANGE: single portion, $3; 6-inch cakes, $11–18; 10-inch cakes, $26–39.50

WEB: www.eileenscheesecake.com

Finding Eileen's is the hard part. But once you've got her coordinates, your cheesecake quest is quite possibly over. It depends upon whether you prefer your cheesecake very heavy, or in Eileen's case, very light, almost chiffon-like, with graham-cracker or chocolate-cookie crust and the subtle tang of sour cream. It sounds simple, but Eileen Avezzano's mother's Russian-Jewish recipe, which Eileen started baking twenty-eight years ago, calls for a variation in the preparation of the batter that insures just such a light, silky texture: the eggs are separated, beaten whites are folded into the cream cheese and sour cream base, then the cake is baked slowly in a water bath. The result has won Eileen awards (rated number one by *The Daily News*) and a wide following throughout the city and beyond. ("It's the Dalai Lama's favorite," Eileen reports, "He always sends someone over for it when he's in town.")

We tried four of the twenty-eight flavors—plain, strawberry (most popular), pineapple, and marble—and loved them all. So do many restaurants, Little Italy cafés, and stores around town who regularly sell Eileen's Special Cheesecake, among them Café Biondo, Garden of Eden, and the Amish Market. The cakes are sold, mostly for takeout, from Eileen's glass-fronted shop, which has a few small café tables. She offers individually baked single servings, whole cakes in 6- and 10-inch sizes, and 10-inch cake halves. Eileen also ships anywhere in the U.S. Don't worry about the overnight delivery; it's best eaten the next day, she says. We agree.

The New York Cheesecake Wars

All around the town, you see signs laying claim to "New York's Best Cheesecake." Certainly cheesecake is the dish most closely associated with the city and the one dearest to its sentimental heart. But what is it exactly? And whose really rates the championship title?

Everybody seems to agree on the essentials: cream cheese, sour cream, egg, and lemon, with a graham-cracker crust. And from there? A friend remembers lunching in the 1950s at The Turf, an old-time prime rib house on Broadway that served wedges of cheesecake "so heavy with cream that the narrow end would bend under the weight as it sat on the plate." The Turf is long gone; so is the original Lindy's, a long-time standard-bearer; and so is any cheesecake that quite lives up to that memory of the 1950s.

Today? The **Carnegie Deli's** (854 Seventh Ave. at 55th St., 212-757-2245) version is tall, creamy-dense, and much loved, as is Junior's, even if it is a little shorter and squatter. We're fans of Eileen's Special Cheese-cake, a decidedly lighter variant, and so are a multitude of admirers. Purists revere the flawless New York cheesecake at **Two Little Red Hens** (1652 Second Ave. at 86th St., 212-452-0476) baked high and handsome. Terrance Brennan's **Artisanal** (35 West 64th St. at Broadway, 212-724-8585) serves up a superb, southern-style praline version; and **Bruno Bakery** (see page 25) goes Italo-Latin with a ricotta-based dulce de leche.

And the winner is . . . ?

elephant & castle

※ *68 Greenwich Avenue bet. Seventh Avenue South and West 11th Street*
PHONE: 212-243-1400
CREDIT CARDS: AmEx, MC, V
PRICE RANGE: crêpes, $6.25–7.50; other, $5.50–7.75

In the 1970s, crêpes were in, then they were out, now they're in again; and all the while Elephant & Castle has stayed the course, retaining all its famous, now retro specialties, of which crêpes were and are prime. The Grand Marnier version stands in for an after-dinner drink; Casablanca is a harmony of vanilla ice cream, banana, and hot fudge; Chestnut crêpe parisienne is a recent addition in which French chestnut purée is deliciously embellished with apricot essence and whipped cream. Then there are those other Castle classics: Boston Indian pudding, whose "secret recipe" of slow-cooked cornmeal and molasses is a veritable time machine for rock-bound yankees; carrot cake that won a "best in New York" twenty years ago (it's holding up nicely); hot fudge sundaes made with Valrhona chocolate; and of course, frou frou, fresh seasonal fruit with Greek yogurt drizzled with Greek honey (made by monks in Crete) or a more secular Vermont maple syrup. Innovations at the Castle include Ciao Bella sorbets and bananas Foster served with sautéed fresh strawberries. Far out.

eleven madison park

※ *11 Madison Avenue at 24th Street*
PHONE: 212-889-0905
CREDIT CARDS; AmEx, MC, V, Disc
PRICE RANGE: $12
WEB: www.elevenmadisonpark.com

"Soaring grandeur" aren't the first words that spring to mind to describe Danny Meyer's other restaurants. Union Square Café, for example, or Gramercy Tavern. But his Eleven Madison Park occupies one of New York's more commanding spaces, with the marble walls, lofty ceiling, and Art Deco details of the former MetLife lobby now softened by masses of flowers, shining silver, and gleaming white napery. If you're having dessert in the raised lounge area, you can look across the airy room and out through the huge windows to vistas of Madison Square Park and the Flatiron Building beyond.

It's glorious. And so are the unfussy, imaginative desserts: an unusual golden pineapple soufflé accented with pecorino and a lemon thyme ice cream; the deeply flavorful Araguani Grand Cru Chocolate Symphony, layered with caramel and a touch of Maldon sea salt; an Earl Grey-vanilla-glazed bosc pear with chestnut mousse and pear sorbet. The menu changes with the seasons and chef Daniel Humm's inspiration, so don't set your heart on one of those—just on having something every bit as good.

One nicely little-known tip: Eleven Madison Park keeps that high and handsome lounge area open straight through the afternoon for light bites and desserts. Play hookey and go; for an hour or so you'll feel you're one of Manhattan's most privileged insiders.

falai panetteria

✣ *79 Clinton Street at Rivington Street*
  PHONE: 212-777-8956
  CREDIT CARDS: AmEx
  PRICE RANGE: $2.50–6

Florence-born Lacopo Falai arrived in New York only in 2001, but quickly became one of our rising-star chefs and the entrepreneurial owner of no less than three eating establishments. Falai Panetteria is just steps from Falai, his namesake restaurant; and Caffe Falai in Soho has become an instant favorite destination for breakfast, lunch, and dinner among that area's locals and tourists alike. Each location offers a savory menu along with Chef Falai's justly famous breads, pastries and desserts, all honed to perfection through years of experience of first working with top talents in Italy and France, then here as executive pastry chef at stellar Le Cirque 2000 and Osteria del Circo. Particularly inviting is the blue-and-white tile décor of the panetteria, with its rococo mirrors, high tin ceiling, striped awning, and ceramic chandeliers that chef Falai was tickled to find at an Italian flea market. Of course, you've come just for dessert—or desserts—as each one just seems to get better and better: the chocolate mousse dome with five-spice cream filling; the delicate almond banana cake made with imported almond flour; the semolina pudding with its fondant of heavy cream and Valhrona chocolate; the strawberry-topped panna cotta. Oh, and there's the bomboloni, the famous Italian vanilla-cream-filled donuts that chef Falai makes with light yeasty brioche dough, and the superb puff pastry cannoli filled with a rum-flavored pudding-like cream. It's a brilliant reinvention of an old favorite. And, like everything chef Falai touches, it's *miracolo*.

caffe emilia

✻ *139 First Avenue at 9th Street*

PHONE: 212-388-1234

CREDIT CARDS: AmEx, MC, V

PRICE RANGE: $5.95

This welcoming café boasts a cool, modernist interior and a tiny garden in which to enjoy Falai breads and desserts, excellent coffee, and espresso—some chocolate-fortified—along with house-made special-ties like a thick chocolate Emilia-Romagnan pudding so rich it turns spoons into gold. We swear.

financier patisserie

❋ *3-4 World Financial Center, Battery Park City*
PHONE: 212-786-3220

❋ *35 Cedar Street at 10 Liberty Plaza bet. Pearl and William Streets*
PHONE: 212-952-3838
CREDIT CARD: AmEx, MC, V
PRICE RANGE: pastries, $3.25–4.25; tarts, 6-inch, $14, 9-inch, $24; cakes, $24.50–39.50
WEB: www.financierpastries.com

When a French gourmet enters a patisserie for the first time, he orders an éclair. The theory is, if the éclair is good, every-thing else will be, too.

The éclairs at Financier (pronounced "fee-NAHN-cee-ay"), one an intense coffee cream in pâte-à-choux pastry with a sticky glaze of caramel running its length, are among the city's very best. The same can be said for all the twenty-five or thirty choices spread before your dazzled eyes. A *religieuse*, sel-dom seen and never forgotten. Small strawberry passionfruit cakes with the strawberries nestled in the mousse. A plum tart, its fresh plums resting on a butter cream beneath a crum-bly top. "The best macarons I've ever had," in one friend's words. And with your coffee comes a miniature *financier* (shaped like a little gold brick, hence the name), an irresistible almond sponge cake that the patisserie also sells a few thou-sand of each week.

Chef Eric Bedoucha prides himself on his adherence to classic standards, with perhaps the smallest concessions to his own tastes. (The layers of coffee butter cream, chocolate ganache, and almond sponge cake beneath a deep chocolate glaze in his opera stand perhaps 1/8-inch higher than their French ancestors, he admits.)

Now expanded to three financial-district locations, the original—looking out on a cobblestone street—is still our favorite. With its immaculate appointments—tile flooring, pastel walls, comfortable faux-bamboo chairs—Financier would fit into any smart European street, from Paris to Rome to Copenhagen.

When Dessert is a Very Special Cake

Whether for weddings or birthdays or other special occasions, a gorgeous or amazingly decorated cake is often at the top of the want list (and should probably be in the pre-nup). Many bakeries discussed in this book will oblige with fabulous, custom-made creations—Payard and Fauchon spring to mind, along with Black Hound, and Cupcake Café. But here are more New York specialty bakers whose artistry with sugar and buttercream can interpret your wildest or most romantic fantasies: **Colette's Cakes** (681 Washington St. bet. West 10th and Charles Sts., 212-366-6530, www.colettescakes.com) for whimsical designs and finishes. **Creative Cakes** (400 East 74th St. bet. First and Second Aves., 212-794-9811, www.creativecakesny.com) for funky and fun conversation pieces. **Sylvia Weinstock Cakes** (273 Church St. bet. Franklin and Watts Sts., 212-925-6698, www.sylviaweinstock.com) for magnificent cakes with the most convincing trompe-l'oeil flowers. Most bakers are by appointment only for special orders.

good enough to eat

❊ *483 Amsterdam Avenue bet. 83rd and 84th Streets*
PHONE: 212-496-0163
CREDIT CARDS: AmEx, MC, V
PRICE RANGE: cake slices, $6; pie slices, $5.50–6;
brownies, squares, and cookies, $2–6
WEB: www.goodenoughtoeat.com

"We bake all day and all night," says Carrie Levin, chef and owner of this homey neighborhood restaurant known for bountiful breakfasts and classic all-American food at lunch and dinner. The pastry case is filled with chocolate, carrot, and coconut layer cakes; fruit, pumpkin, and pecan pies; crisps, squares, brownies, and cookies—in short, all the comfy desserts Levin remembers from childhood. But she learned her baking skills in Brussels, where her parents lived for a time in her youth. "It's where the best bakeries are," says Levin, who uses only Belgian chocolate, and on Tuesday nights prepares a special Belgian dessert: orange-almond-Grand Marnier cake.

In 1981, Levin opened Good Enough, dedicating her restaurant to "good, old-fashioned American food." Her baked goods, made with the assistance of Michelle Weber, have an avid following. One customer, who comes in regularly for a slice of Levin's scrumptious coconut layer cake with rich cream cheese frosting showered with shredded coconut, was so upset when Levin once changed the filling to lemon custard that the original recipe was immediately reinstated. Another neighborhood denizen calls the strawberry pie "to die for" and we found the pumpkin smooth and perfectly textured. If there's any doubt that New Yorkers need home-style desserts now more than ever, Levin points to the fact that after September 11, 2001, her weekly flour order increased from 700 to 1,000 pounds.

~~~~~~

gotham bar & grill

❋ *12 East 12th Street bet. Fifth Avenue and University Place*
PHONE: 212-620-4020
CREDIT CARDS: AmEx, MC, V, Disc
PRICE RANGE: $12
WEB: www.gothambarandgrill.com

Who said good things don't last? Almost two decades have passed since Alfred Portale first began piling plates high with his trail-blazing ventures into contemporary American cuisine. And he's still rousing the palates and passions of New York's gourmet cognoscenti, afternoons and evenings, at his landmark Gotham Bar & Grill. The room is a wide-open space, minimally and boldly conceived. The magic is in the attention to detail—like those ebonized maple trays that define your individual place at the bar. The same can be said for pastry chef Deborah Racicot's precisionist, lick-the-plate flavorful desserts: strawberry shortcake paired with a white chocolate mousse, enlivened with a dash of twelve-year aged balsamic; apricot crisp lightened with a goat-cheese-lavender crème caramel; a multisensation roasted fig and currant tart with a sprinkling of brazil nuts and a scoop of marsala sorbet; the once-and-for-always Gotham chocolate cake, made young again with a scoop of chicory ice cream. This is an especially nice destination after the theater, when the crowds have gone and the tables are open to all.

Grand Central Market
❄ Lexington Avenue at 43rd Street
PHONE: 212-340-2347
WEB: www.grandcentralterminal.com

Whether you find yourself in Grand Central Station as a commuter or come to admire its architectural splendor as a visitor, you should know about Grand Central Market—and the multitude of desserts it offers.

The street-level Grand Central Market arcade starts at the Lexington Avenue and 43rd Street end of the station with **Corrado** (212-599-4321), where you'll find apple turnovers, prune Danish, and other pastries ($4–4.50), whole cakes ($19–25), tea cakes ($2.50), and cookies. **Zaro's** (212-292-0160, www.zaro.com) here and at three other locations in the Terminal, has many kinds of fresh whole cakes ($12.95–15.95), including carrot, cheese, and fruit tortes, but slices only at their shop near Track 34. Also in the Market hall, look for **Li-Lac's** (212-370-4866, www.li-lacchocolates.com) chocolate-covered oreos and grahams ($1.10 & $2.20), kiddie pops ($.45), and pralines ($1.85); and, at **Godiva Chocolatiers** (212-808-0276, www.godiva.com), biscotti and chocolate-covered biscuits. On the lower dining concourse **Junior's** (212-692-9800, www.juniors cheesecake.com) provides a full-service restaurant and retail bakery where you can have a sit-down meal and/or a piece of the famous cheesecake to go in all nine variations and sizes (Little Fella-size: $2.95). Also on the Concourse, **Ciao Bella** (www.ciaobella.com) goes well beyond simple cups and cones (bambini one-scoop $3.45 for kids 12 and under; $4.75 otherwise) with shakes and smoothees ($5.95–6.95) and gelato-filled crêpes ($4.95–9.50). All the scrumptious pies, individual cheesecakes, and teacakes available at **Little Pie Company**'s other branches are also here to be sampled (see also page 70).

gramercy tavern

❋ *42 East 20th Street bet. Broadway and Park Avenue South*

PHONE: 212-477-0777

CREDIT CARDS: AmEx, MC, V, Disc

PRICE RANGE: $8

WEB: www.gramercytavern.com

Chocolate peanut-butter cake with frozen milk. Warm apple crisp with vanilla and cinnamon ice creams and Caramel Sauce. Warm chocolate bread pudding with cacao nib ice cream. Plum upside-down cake with Armagnac crème anglaisé, and plum sorbet. Pastry chef Nancy Olson grew up on a farm in North Dakota, and her mouth-watering pastries are rooted in her childhood. Using farm-fresh, seasonal ingredients, she creates confections that are at once homey, full-flavored, and elegant. The roomy, convivial Tavern Room with its rustic-urban decor will accommodate you for dessert-only dining (we like it better than the more formal dining room anyway). And, as a nice courtesy, it doesn't discriminate between diners and desserters. No reservations are taken. Prepare to wait for your reward along with everyone else.

grom

✣ *2165 Broadway at 76th Street*
PHONE: 646-290-7233
CREDIT CARDS: AmEx, V
PRICE RANGE: cones and cups, $4.75–$9; packaged, $8,
$12, $24
WEB: www.grom.it

The coffee gelato at Grom is so good, so intensely flavored and creamy, you'll wish you could have it for breakfast every day. Incidentally, having Grom's gelato for breakfast—the store opens at 11 a.m.—is the best way to avoid the line that forms later in the day in front of this *buonissima e deliziosa* new gelateria. Grom opened its first shop outside of Italy in 2007 and became an instant phenomenon in Manhattan, despite (or maybe because of) the top-price offerings. The establishment is named for one of its two owners, Federico Grom, who partnered with Piedmontese winemaker Guido Martinetti to create a product made from the highest quality, fresh seasonal ingredients—drawn from Italy and elsewhere—using methods that reflect the care given to wine production. All the fruits, nuts, creams, chocolates, sugars, even water, are selected and hand-processed in Grom's Turin factory. The base mixtures are shipped frozen and creamed on site. Grom uses San Bernardo mineral water for all its sorbets, organic eggs, and whole milk from a cooperative to create, in the owners' words, "*il gelato comme volta*" (ice cream as it used to be). Customers at Grom's small takeout store (there are four tables) may sample several different flavors before making the big decision from the twenty flavors available. And it's hard, hard, we tell you. The quality of Italy's fruits and nuts is legendary, so in choosing, say, the lemon sorbet, you are really tasting the famous thick-skinned, low-acid lemons from Amalfi. The mandarin orange is made with Sicilian Ciaculli late-winter mandarins, a citrus of sweet perfection. On our first visit we also sampled several different chocolate flavors: one that tingled in the mouth with candied orange zest; a Gianduja, redolent of intense Piedmontese hazelnuts; and Extra Noir, a deep, dark chocolate made with Ecuadorian chocolate chips. As word spreads, the line will undoubtedly get longer, so plan on that morning "coffee," an espresso-based flavor made with Guatemalan beans "lightly softened with a small amount of cream," soon. We can tell you how remarkable it is, but tasting is the true wake-up call.

Molto Gelato

New York has no shortage of gelaterias. Among the finest is our own home-grown **Il Laboratorio del Gelato** (95 Orchard St. bet. Broome and Delancey Sts., 212-343-9922, www.laboratoriodelgelato.com), whose unusual and delicious flavors are served in its little take-out shop, as well as in restaurants throughout the city, and sold packaged at Whole Foods Union Square, Dean and Deluca, and Murray's Cheese. We keep coming back for pear sorbet, caramel, and the scrumptious Divini—frozen gelati truffles with crunchy coatings. With six locations around the city **Ciao Bella Cafés** (www.ciaobellagelato.com) make it easy to keep current with the old and new flavors, such as the always wonderful blood orange sorbet, and the seasonal pumpkin and spice gelato. **Gelato Dei Presidi** (see page 37) is easy to miss, but don't, not with flavors like puckery sweet mandarin, and bacio (chocolate hazelnut) , all made with Italian ingredients. See also **Otto** (page 78) and **Sant Ambroeus** (page 90).

houston's

❉ *378 Park Avenue South at 27th Street*
PHONE: 212-689-1090
CREDIT CARDS: AmEx, MC, V
PRICE RANGE: $8
WEB: www.hillstone.com

Looking for a pleasant, out-of-New-York-like American experience? Houston's is just the destination—a non-edgy oasis that feels positively Midwestern compared to its flashier, trendier Park Avenue South neighbors.

One reason is that this Houston's is a branch of the successful restaurant chain that stretches across the continent. If they have a formula, it's one a lot of New Yorkers have taken to their hearts. (Lines can be long at peak hours.)

For starters, Houston's couldn't be friendlier, with staffers who'll seat and serve you with a smile—even if you order just dessert. The bonus: Everyone, not just your designated wait person, watches out for you. The atmosphere is more relaxed lounge than bustling eatery: dim light, deep colors, and lots of snuggly booths and wraparound banquettes available to all. (One unworldly couple, babe in arms, got prime seating when we visited.)

The desserts are a perfect fit. Beyond some Edy's ice cream, they number just three, each a perfectly executed version of an American classic. We went for the key lime pie enthusiastically recommended by friends, but that's strictly a summer special. Always on the menu is the many-splendored five-nut brownie, with vanilla ice cream, gussied up with a creamy champagne sauce. The cheesecake is tall and smo-o-o-th. Apple crumble is buttery, with the balance happily tilting toward more walnuts than most restaurateurs want to shell out for.

Like every Houston's, this one has its own dedicated

dessert chef in the kitchen, baking with prime ingredients. Chain? It's a far cry from bearded colonels and golden arches.

houston's citygroup center

✳ *153 East 53rd Street at Lexington Avenue*
PHONE: 212-888-3828

Same menu. Same smiling service. To our minds a little less welcoming in its below-ground location. But don't let that hold you back. The happy throngs don't seem to mind at all.

hungarian pastry shop

✳ *1030 Amsterdam Avenue at 111th Street*
PHONE: 212-866-4230
CASH ONLY
PRICE RANGE: pastries and slices, $1.75–2.75; cakes, $25 and up

Walk a few steps inside the door and it's not hard to imagine you've time-traveled back to a student café near the university in Old Budapest: plain wooden tables and chairs worn with age in the low-ceilinged room in back, the low hum of students debating art and philosophy and cybergenetics. Cybergenetics? Well, these students are from Columbia, just up Amsterdam Avenue, and this is one of their hangouts.

Hungarian Pastry Shop is one of the last places in New York offering the full range of indigenous Hungarian desserts, along with the specialties it shares with its European neighbors: hearty strudels (in four varieties), Linzertorte, Sacher torte, Dobostorte, Stefania, goosefoot cake—all listed above the counter where you place your order and pick up your food. It's not fancy, but it's authentic. Budapest-trained chef Zoltan Bona uses all butter, along with quality ingredients that he gathers through his own sources, like the poppyseeds oozing from the overfilled poppyseed strudel, and the cocoa and chocolate that combine to make a blissful Rigo Janci.

It all makes the perfect ending to a mini-*mittel European* outing: an amble around Columbia's lovely campus or Morningside Park—then a relaxing sojourn at one of Hungarian Pastry Shop's sidewalk tables, gazing at the soaring spires of the Cathedral of St. John the Divine, just across the avenue. Total cost: less than $10. Ah, Budapest.

le pain quotidien

See website for locations: www.lepainquotidien.com
CREDIT CARDS: AmEx, MC, V
PRICE RANGE: brownies and mini tarts, $3.25-5.50; large
fruit tarts and mousse cakes, $24.95

This Belgian coffee house chain, with thirty locations throughout Europe, is known for excellent breads (the name means "daily bread"), but also for cakes and pastries, most of which are baked at the Mercer Street kitchen for its New York outlets. Executive Chef Ari Cohen presides over everything from baguettes, rolls, and croissants to organic vegan muffins, airy Belgian-style brownies, almond pound cake with orange peel, a variety of fruit tarts, and the subtle chestnut-cream-filled Mont Blanc with a chocolate truffle hidden in the center. At Pain Quotidien the atmosphere is rustic European. Customers sit at long communal farmhouse tables to enjoy soups, sandwiches, salads, and of course dessert, confident that almost all ingredients used, from flours to locally grown fruits, are organic and that famed Belgian chocolate is used exclusively. The SoHo location features a spectacular glass wall that separates the front counter from the dining room, a dramatic space that can be reserved for special occasions.

little pie company

❈ *424 West 43rd Street bet 9th and 10th Avenues*
PHONE: 212-736-4780
CREDIT CARDS: AmEx, MC, V, Disc
PRICE RANGE: pie slices, $3.50; 5-inch pies, $6; 8-inch pies, $14–18; 10-inch pies, $20–26; cake slices, $3.50; cakes, $4–27
WEB: www.littlepiecompany.com
Also available in Grand Central Terminal, lower dining concourse; 212-983-3538

A good pie is hard to find, but not at LPC, with its ten flaky variations. Most of the fruit pies use an old-fashioned butter-and-lard crust, the kind you find at country fairs. The tender cherry is filled with slightly tart Montmorency cherries from an orchard in upstate New York—mercifully, no cornstarch thickener is used. The sweet and chunky sour cream apple walnut has a butter apple-cider cinnamon crust filled with Granny Smiths and topped with a brown-sugar streusel, and the meltingly good banana cream coconut is layered with a cloud of sweetened whipped cream. The seasonal Key lime pie made with sweetened condensed milk has a waiting list. LPC also makes old-fashioned cakes (including applesauce carrot, New York-style cheesecakes, and cupcakes) that can be enjoyed at the stores with espresso, cappuccino, or a latte.

Dessert on Wheels

First, the buzz of the intercom, then that beautiful word: Delivery! Dessert is on the way—think the absolutely freshest cookies, the fudgiest brownies, the tangiest "lemon lemon" bars (you *can't* eat just one), the most tender mini linzer tarts and caramely mini schnecken— all courtesy of master baker Seth Greenberg, scion of New York's iconic baking family. **Seth Greenberg's Just Desserts** may be pricey (hefty brownies, $28 per dozen; old-world cookies, $40 per pound), but the home-baked texture and delicate flavors will exceed your expectations, whether for parties or just to thrill your inner cookie connoisseur. (Phone orders only: 646-290-9204, no shipping; minimum order is a dozen, or by the pound, plus $15 delivery charge; available throughout Manhattan and lower Westchester).

"Say it with flour," is the tagline for **Dessert Delivery** (360 East 55th St. at First Ave., phone orders only: 212-838-5411, www.dessertdeliveryny.com), a company that hurtles through the streets of Gotham with truckloads of precious sugar-and-flour cargo to lay at your doorstep: specialty cakes of all kinds, party cakes, fruit pies, pastries and more. The extensive menu and reasonable prices ($25 minimum, plus delivery; no shipping) make this a go-to company for locally made goodies and gifts, suitable for parties small and large.

Kim Ima's mobile bakery **The Treats Truck** (212-691-5226; www.treatstruck.com) parks Monday through Saturday throughout Manhattan and Brooklyn, but Kim will also deliver right to your door bringing the goodies you need and love. Log on either to place a special order or to check out her various parking locations. The pecan butterscotch bar—not to mention the raspberry brownie—is reason enough to hoof it to any of Kim's hard-won parking spots (her heart-rending parking travails are posted on the website and well worth an empathetic read). Kim's truck Sugar, by the way, runs on compressed natural gas, keeping her carbon footprint way down, and her "delicious" quotient up, all at modest prices.

The haute **DessertTruck** (www.desserttruck.com) parks at 8th Street and University Place (6 p.m. to midnight, weekends from noon) dispensing luxury ($5) treats both chilled (Madagascan crème brulée; milk chocolate mousse with a peanut butter cream center and carmelized popcorn) and warm (carmelized banana sandwich; molten chocolate cake with Spanish olive oil, pistachios, and sea salt), offered "for those looking for a new experience"—all the work of Jerome Chang, a former pastry sous chef at Le Cirque.

The Waffle Truck (www.wafelsanddinges.com) is the brainchild of genuine Belgian Thomas DeGeest, who makes genuine Belgian waffles ($4 and $7)—big, fluffy and sweet—with luscious dinges (toppings): whipped cream and strawberries, of course, but chocolate and maple syrup too ($1). Check website for locations, and for the secret word, which will earn you a free dinge when spoken at point of purchase.

minamoto kitchoan

❖ *608 Fifth Avenue at 49th Street*
PHONE: 212-489-3747
CREDIT CARDS: AmEx, MC, V

PRICE RANGE: rice cake, $2.50; jellies, $3.50–4; seasonal winter persimmon jellies, $11; winter chestnut jellies, $8
WEB: www.kitchoan.com

Step through the doors of Minamoto Kitchoan and put aside all tired ideas of what a sweet shop can be. Here you'll find *wagashi*, traditional Japanese confections, exquisitely wrapped and arranged like a display of museum still lifes: a ripe, stemmed cherry suspended in transparent jelly; a walnut-filled rice cake coated with vivid green powder wrapped to look like a purple Japanese iris; or the confection known as *yoshinozakura*, a boiled sweet made with actual essence of cherry blossoms and wrapped in pink, petal-shaped paper. It's available very briefly in the spring, when the cherry trees are in bloom. These are the most refined and exotic sweets on the planet, an acquired taste, to be sure, but a must for intrepid dessert lovers who would like expand their horizons. Wagashi ingredients include jelly (made from arrowroot; no animal products are used), red bean paste, yam, and rice flour. Every form is inspired by nature and intended to engage all five senses: sight, taste, touch, scent, but also sound, as in when you hear the name of the pastry spoken. Here, every offering has a descriptive note, and there's a brochure to guide you further—perhaps to having a wagashi tasting party for your more sophisticated friends.

soba-ya
❊ *229 East 9th Street at Second Avenue*
PHONE: 212-533-6966

The Japanese noodle house **Soba-Ya** is the unlikely source of some of the best Asian ice cream flavors in town. We love the sweet-and-pungent honey wasabi, the nutty black sesame, and yuza sorbet, named for the mildly tangy Japanese lime. We differed over the powerful green tea that one of us thought was too bitter, but the other loved. Three flavors to a plate for $5.

once upon a tart

❖ *135 Sullivan Street bet. Houston and Prince Streets*

PHONE: 212-387-8869

CREDIT CARDS: AmEx, MC, V, Disc

PRICE RANGE: small tarts, $5.50; savories, $5.35–16.50; 7-inch fruit tarts, $15.50

WEB: www.onceuponatart.com

In their cookbook, *Once upon a Tart,* owners Frank Mentesana and Jerome Audureau tell the story of their shop's phenomenal success as a prime savory and sweet tart destination. Their search for the perfect space led them to 135 Sullivan Street, a beat-up looking storefront that had in fact been a bakery a hundred years earlier. The cluttered basement revealed the original fixtures, glass pedestals, and shelving still intact. Once cleaned up and installed, these vintage touches are now an integral part of the quaint interior space with bright yellow walls, pressed tin ceilings, and not just tarts on display. Breakfast and lunch are served daily to a loyal clientele (one customer comes in every morning for two scones, one for him and one for his dog), but for the dessert connoisseur, the sweet tarts, freshly baked on premises with delicate butter crust, are the main attraction. The flavors change seasonally and the fruit tarts emphasize the freshness of whatever is ripe and best at the moment—plums, peaches, blueberries, pears. The chocolate pear tart we sampled was a lovely mélange of textures and flavors: delicate butter crust, rich chocolate cream, and ripe fruit. What more could you ask for?

Greenmarket

Twenty-seven locations within Manhattan
Phone for locations, days, and hours: 212-477-3220

On a balmy spring, summer, fall, or, for the hardy, winter day, do what the chefs do: Go to the Greenmarket.

New Yorkers often come back from visits to Europe raving about the bowls of extraordinary fresh fruits so often brought to the table as dessert in sunny climates like Italy and Spain. It's an experience you can easily duplicate with freshly harvested, high-quality produce you buy directly from the folks who grow it in New York's neighboring rural areas: plump, juicy, tree- and vine-ripened strawberries, raspberries, plums, peaches, melons, and pears.

Twenty-seven greenmarkets are scattered around Manhattan alone, most open one or two days a week. The official starting time for most of them is 8 a.m. and if you want the pick of the crop, the earlier you get there, the better. Remember, you're competing with all those high-ranking chefs, each casting eagle eyes over what will become the seasonal specialties they take such pride in.

The largest and most famous greenmarket is the one at Union Square, open four days a week, where early-morning shopping is almost a blood sport. As at its citywide siblings, you can also find locally made cheeses, ciders, jams, and pastries. "No fat; no sugar" is the claim to greatness made by many of the bakers, with about the results you've come to recognize. A notch above are seasonal fruit pies with delicate crusts from Breezy Hill Orchards and, from Hawthorne Valley Farm, rich brownies and big chocolate chip and ginger cookies.

osteria del circo

❖ *120 West 55th Street bet. Sixth and Seventh Avenues*
PHONE: 212-265-3636
CREDIT CARDS: AmEx, MC, V, Disc
PRICE RANGE: $6–10; tasting menu, $12
WEB: www.osteriadelcirco.com

For "Ladies and Gentlemen, Boys and Girls of All Ages," Osteria del Circo introduces itself on its website. That gives you some idea of the pleasure principle at work in this lighter-hearted sibling of Le Cirque 2000.

Both restaurants are the pampered creations of the ebullient Maccioni family, and we doubt there's a time when you won't find at least one of them on hand, ringmastering the proceedings.

The carnival tent atmosphere was designed by Adam Tihany: gold stars hanging from the ceiling, sculptured monkeys frolicking near the striped pole, a trapeze sailing over the bar.

Even the desserts come on festive hand-painted ceramic plates. And, yes, the desserts are festive, too, inspired versions of Maccioni family favorites: the famous *bomboloncini* (light Tuscan doughnuts) come filled with a variety of creams. Cannoli shells are stuffed with their chocolate-and-hazelnut-flecked ricotta cream just before being rushed to your table, so they're still crunchy. You can even indulge in the original crème brûlée Le Cirque, the standard by which all others have since been judged.

The Maccionis will smilingly lead you to a just-for-dessert table in the dining room if one is available. Call ahead, or just stop by and ask.

le cirque

�֍ *151 East 58th Street at Lexington Avenue*
PHONE: 212-644-0202
CREDIT CARDS: AmEx, MC, V, Disc
PRICE RANGE: $12–15
WEB: www.lecirque.com

For a real taste of culinary history (at a tab below three figures), betake yourself to the opulent bar at this lengendary temple of haute cuisine. Le Cirque has now relocated from the stately old Vuillard rooms on Madison Avenue to a luxury, ultra-modern high rise. But inside it retains the gilded grandeur of the original—the ultimate setting in which to enjoy that crème brûlée with which Papa Maccioni first thrilled New Yorkers, a paper-thin crisp of browned sugar over a pool of ambrosian custard. It's just one of a dozen choices, including such classics as crêpes suzette, Baked Alaska, and the tour-de-force chocolate Le Cirque Stove. They don't make desserts like that anymore? They do at Le Cirque.

After the Theater

"We don't go out for dessert after the theater," a grumpy know-it-all informed us. "They won't give you just dessert."

Is he ever wrong! And what a pleasure he's depriving himself of!

Concerning the "wrong" part: Even the chicest, most heavily booked restaurants are likely to welcome you with open arms after 10:30 or so, in this increasingly early-to-bed city. Chelsea's small and thriving **Red Cat**, for one, couldn't quite promise they'd give up seats for dessert-only at the prime-time dinner hours. But later? Sure, especially during the week.

Again, our best advice is to call ahead and ask, if you can. If you can't, just show up and smile. It's worked for us every time.

Obviously it's a pleasure, whether you're prolonging the high of a great evening of theater or compensating for a bummer. The bonus: By the time you finish dessert, it'll be easier to get a cab.

otto

✣ *1 Fifth Avenue at 8th Street*
PHONE: 212-995-9559
CREDIT CARDS: AmEx, MC, V, Disc
PRICE RANGE: $7–9
WEB: www.ottopizzeria.com

The designer pizzas and "little plates" have brought their own crowds to Otto, but for dessert cognoscenti the draw is definitely the gelato. How much art and craft can go into the making of gelato? Chef Meredith Kurtzman went to Italy to learn. And the knowledge she returned with—coupled with her own creative imagination—will have you shamelessly piling up the plates on your table.

Of course, you have to try the olive oil gelato (you'll taste a touch of sea salt), served with tart blood oranges in a wine syrup. It's a conversation-stopper, but don't mix and match it with the ever-changing fantasy of sweeter offerings. Most popular, with reason, is the goat cheese ricotta gelato, combined with wine-poached mission figs and candied walnuts. We loved a banana gelato, drizzled with chocolate sauce and dried cherries, and a vanilla gelato with tangerine sorbet and meringue.

A few flavors, including a not-to-be-ignored hazelnut stracciatella, grace the printed menu. But it's essential that you inquire about that day's gelato specials. You can get basic two- or three-gelato tasting plates, but those are just teases.

The narrow dark-wood room beyond the bar leads into a brighter, more open room looking out on Washington Mews, and regulars include art-smart locals, a number with toddlers and strollers during our midday visits. Everyone looks happy, knowing they can promenade away the pounds along the historic northern border of Washington Square with its row of elegant, nineteenth-century, Henry James-era houses.

payard patisserie & bistro

❖ *1032 Lexington Avenue bet. 73rd and 74th Streets*
PHONE: 212-717-5252
CREDIT CARDS: AmEx, MC, V
PRICE RANGE: fancy pastries, $6; bistro desserts, $7–11

On any given Saturday, Payard is packed and buzzing with stylish customers enjoying light snacks and pastries in the front patisserie, or multicourse lunches in the quieter, dark-paneled bistro dining room. (A tea menu is also offered from 3:30 to 5 p.m. Monday through Saturday.) It seems the perfect place to indulge oneself, after a morning of gallery going or shopping, with the best of French pastry and bistro fare. Owner (with Daniel Boulud) and patissier is Francois Payard while Philippe Bertineau presides over the bistro menu that offers its own composed desserts—upside-down bittersweet dark chocolate soufflé with pistachio ice cream, for example, or verbena and raspberry crème brûlée. An exclusively dessert-oriented visit will get you seated in the front room, after you've had a good look at the fancy pastries on display. All the classic French pastries are here in Payard's particular and meticulous rendition, along with exquisite fruit tarts, napoleons (we sampled the impossibly delicate raspberry version), éclairs, entire cakes (the domed Le Louvre is a popular chocolate-hazelnut creation), and across the room, Payard's own chocolates. At holiday time, Payard sells cake-decorating kits for kids ($25), and for your wedding they'll create a gorgeous, multitiered cake that you'll spend the rest of your life living up to. Whatever your pleasure, it will assuredly be provided with that soupçon of elegance that makes true French style.

podunk

❊ *231 East 5th Street bet. Second Avenue and Cooper Square*

PHONE: 212-677-7722

CASH ONLY

PRICE RANGE: cookies, $0.75; cupcakes, $1.50; cake slices, $2.75–3.75; teas for two, $22–30; children's tea, $8; birthday tea, $10 per participant; student tea for one, $8

Elspeth Treadwell's self-described tearoom/coffeehouse/bakery is usually fragrant with the aroma of freshly baked cardamom cake, a Scandinavian specialty served with a choice of apricot-ginger or cayenne-lingonberry sauces. "We start from scratch and bake all day," she says. "People love the 'warm from the oven' aspect of what they come across each time they visit." Warm as well is Treadwell's friendly presence as she jogs between front counter and kitchen, whipping up everything from cupcakes and cookies to layer cakes, buttery scones, and savories. While you are welcome to order one or more of anything with tea, coffee, cappuccino, or espresso, Podunk also offers eight different tea menus that include both savories and sweets: smorgasbord, chocolate, rustic, nibbler, and cookie, as well as a children's milk-and-cupcake tea, which becomes a birthday tea with the addition of a birthday layer cake plus candles. Podunk is exceptionally kid-friendly—sitting on the floor is totally acceptable, for grownups too—and the atmosphere is of a country antiquesshop, which in fact it is. All the furniture, Treadwell's passionately acquired collection of rustic country pieces, is for sale. "Regular customers get angry when their favorite chair is sold," she says. Pre-Podunk, Treadwell was an "office person, in cubicles all my life." With the opening of her charming little storefront tea room in 2002, she's realized a dream—that of pulling together everything she cares about: baking, antiques, and a country way of life. Podunk, she has said, is where she's from.

poseidon bakery

❉ *629 Ninth Avenue bet. 44th and 45th Streets*
PHONE: 212-757-6173
CREDIT CARDS: MC, V
PRICE RANGE: pastries, $1.85–2.10; cookies, $11.95/lb; strudel, $8.25/lb

Has the west side of Ninth Avenue been designated a land-mark area? It gets our vote. In a few blocks in the 40s you can still find old-fashioned, no-frill purveyors of some of the fresh-est fish and greatest cheeses in New York and, at Poseidon Bakery, the finest Greek pastries, bar none.

Phyllo dough is the one essential in the best-known of the Greek pastries, and Poseidon is the last pastry shop in the city that makes its own, fresh, every day—light, flaky, tender. In Poseidon's baklava, it folds around beautifully balanced layers of walnuts and almonds, drenched in a cinnamon-spiced honey-based syrup. In trigana, it surrounds an almond paste triangle. Kombehaye is a light fluffy sponge cake wrapped in phyllo.

Look around, and pick what appeals to you. Everything is described; and if one of the third- or fourth-generation family members is at the counter—Tony, Lily, or their son Paul—they'll go into enthusiastic detail. We loved the galac-toburiko, a rich custard pastry, and kourambiedes, butter almond cookies in a snowfall of powdered sugar. The mixed-nut brittle is sensational.

Don't be surprised at the unassuming atmosphere. This is a mom-and-pop (and -son) operation; they put their time and money into first-rate ingredients and TLC, as they have for decades.

A Taste of Honey and More

There's more to Greek and Middle Eastern desserts than baklava. The Egyptian owned **Melange Food Fair** (1277 First Ave. bet. 68th & 69th Sts., 212-535-7773) is a reliable source both for *katayifi*, the crunchy nut-filled shredded wheat pie, and *besbousa*, the Moroccan semolina honey cake sprinkled with rose water and almonds. Take the 7 train to Astoria for a deep immersion into Greek and Middle Eastern culture—and sweets—stopping at **Laziza** (25-78 Steinway St. at 28th St., Queens, 718-777-7676), an immaculate and popular bakery that sells—along with multiple variations of honey-drenched phyllo pastries—the Palestinian sweetened cheese pie *knafe*, served warm; and don't overlook their large selection of appealing date-filled and sesame-sprinkled cookies. At **Omonia Café** (32-20 Broadway at 33rd St., Queens, 718-274-6650), a spacious, two-level restaurant with a lavish pastry and dessert display up front, owner Yani Arvanitis makes excellent versions of two European-style custard-cream Greek cakes: *ekmek*, topped with a layer of chantilly cream and fresh sliced almonds—light and delicious—and his own version of *galacto boureko*, a cream-filled phyllo pastry in light syrup and dusted with pure cinnamon—we ate the whole thing. No special order is too big for Omonia, whose seven-chef bakery prides itself on having made the cake for the movie *My Big Fat Greek Wedding*.

quintessence

❖ *263 East 10th Street bet. First Avenue and Avenue A*

PHONE: 646-654-1804

CREDIT CARDS: AmEx, MC, V

PRICE RANGE: $8-10; platter, $18

WEB: www.raw-q.com

How about a trip to the cutting edge? For extreme vegans, "raw" is where it's at, and Quintessence is the best place we've found to get a taste. At Quintessence nothing is cooked or baked—from appetizers to desserts—and the results are a revelation.

We went to Quintessence—with its coolly relaxing minimalist interior—to experience an entire raw meal, with a special anticipation of desserts that friends had recommended. The desserts are mainly pies with crusts made from a dense, ground, tasty mixture of soaked almonds, soaked walnuts and apricots with other flavorings. Their coconut pie's carob-nut crust is filled with young, creamy "live" coconut. It was exceptionally light and subtle, and though interesting, we preferred the more intense pecan pie made with raw pecans and fresh dates—the surprisingly predominant flavor. We also sampled a fine mango-peach pie with organic chocolate topping and a deliciously fresh fruit plate. The three-layer mudslide pie featuring layers of pecan fudge carob mousse and mesquite cream in an almond-walnut crust is understandably one of the most popular desserts on the menu.

Vegan and Raw: Good-for-you Desserts

Desserts made without butter, eggs or even sugar? Why bother? a true dessert lover might ask. But vegan and raw baking have come of age, with tasty choices that can turn skeptics into believers. Vegan desserts are made with plant-based ingredients only; no dairy products of any kind are used. Raw "baking" takes it even further: no ingredient is heated above 118-degrees F in order to preserve the enzymes and nutrients, or so the adherents believe. If you're just learning about all of this, **Babycakes** (248 Broome St. at Ludlow St., 212 677-5047, www.babycakesnyc.com), which calls itself an allergen-free bakery (most items are gluten-, dairy-, egg-, soy-, and sugar-free), is a good place to start. Cupcakes, cookies, and muffins all bear ingredient labels (agave nectar is the sweetener) and the staff helpfully explains each product, if you ask. Our favorite is the carrot cupcake, a delicious wheat-free treat with creamy vanilla icing. The decadent richness of the nine different kinds of vegan cakes at rock star Moby's **Teany** (90 Rivington St. bet. Ludlow and Orchard Sts., 212-475-9190, www.teany.com) is belied by their healthful ingredients. We love the chocolate peanut-butter mousse cake (a candy bar gone to heaven); but don't ignore the dense chocolate-coconut macaroon cake, or the light tofu-based cheesecake garnished with fresh fruit. Teany's cakes are shipped in from Vegan Treats (www.vegan treats.com), a small Pennsylvania bakery, while the scones (black currant, orange cranberry, cherry pecan) and quick breads (zucchini and pumpkin) are made by local bakers, all to be enjoyed in a charming tearoom setting. Everything at **Pure Juice and Take-away** (126 East 17th St. at Irving Pl., 212-477-7151, www.oneluckyduck.com), the takeout shop for Sarma Melngailis's Pure Food and Wine restaurant on nearby Irving Place, is made from local and organic ingredients; no dairy, refined sugars, or animal products (with the exception of raw honey) are used. Chocoholics delight in the chocolate pudding (made with cocoa, coconut meat, and agave nectar) and the chocolate tart (cocoa, coconut meat, almonds, and maple syrup). Pure Juice makes its own ice creams using cashew nuts, coconut meat, and agave nectar—try Almond Buttercup, a chocolate almond crunch, and Cacao Chip, a vanilla-chocolate chunk. **LifeThyme** (410 Sixth Ave. bet. 8th and 9th Sts., 212 420-9099, www. lifethymemarket.com) does a brisk business at their all-vegan bakery, selling more than two hundred Toll Booth cookies (crammed with organic chocolate chips and roasted pecan halves) each day, but check out the banana chocolate chip and the apple cinnamon cookies as well. Chief baker Camillo Sabella makes a decadent truffle brownie, a richly caramelized pineapple upside-down cake, a superb strawberry shortcake, and a light cheesecake made with a nut and oat crust and filled with silken tofu. Lifethyme's hamentaschen, rugelach, and strudel are kosher; and any cake or pie can be ordered for special occasions. **Integral Yoga Natural Foods** (229 West 13th St. bet. 7th and 8th Aves., 212-243-2642, www.integralyoganaturalfoods.com) is known for its large selection of raw pies, many made with nut crusts: Cheesecake Lover's pie is the favorite but also good are the Coconut Cream and Louisiana Yam. Integral's vegan desserts include a tofu pumpkin pie, a lemon-strawberry mousse cake, and gluten-free brownies. Try the raw oatmeal raisin cookies, too.

rice to riches

❋ *37 Spring Street bet. Mott and Mulberry Streets*
   PHONE: 212-274-0008
   CREDIT CARDS: AmEx, MC, V, Disc
   PRICE RANGE: 8-ounce solo portion, $5;
   sumo (serves 4), $20
   WEB: www.ricetoriches.com

Rice pudding. End of story. Except that, as served in this futuristic takeout shop, the pudding goes high-concept. Oh yes, they serve the ultimate comfort food in its pristine vanilla form, replete with brown sugar and dark raisins; but then there's Hazelnut Chocolate Bear Hug; Man-made Mascarpone with cherries; and Sex, Drugs, and Rocky Road—in all, over twenty variations (all with jokey names) served cold, with choice of toppings, or warmed on request. We admit to missing some of the earliest flavors, like Bottomless Pear with anise, and Coffee Collapse with a lovely cardamom top note, but the management says their chefs get bored easily. Okay, as long as we have Old Fashioned Romance (traditional) to fall back on we'll put up with Bi-Polar Split Pea (just kidding).

rosa mexicano

❊ *9 East 18th Street bet. Fifth Avenue and Broadway*
   PHONE: 212-533-3350
❊ *1063 First Avenue at 58th Street*
   PHONE: 212-753-7407
❊ *61 Columbus Avenue at 62nd Street*
   PHONE: 212-977-7700
   CREDIT CARDS: MC, V
   PRICE RANGE: $8
   WEB: www.rosamexicano.com

"Dessert is why I get up in the morning," our server Jackie announced (we asked) on the day we visited this restaurant's Union Square location. Our sentiments exactly. Pastry chef Alma Quino presides here with a deft hand that delivers some of the city's most delectable Mexican-accented specialties: a light, custardy, coconut-flecked flan, garnished with a candied cilantro leaf for nibbling. The creamy cheesecake, caramel goat's milk dulce de leche bursting from the center, while a blackberry-chili sauce encircles the whole. The warm chocolate soufflé cake that comes, amazingly, with a little pitcher of sweet-and-tart tomatillo sauce infused with passionfruit. (To eat: punch a hole in the molten soufflé, pour in the sauce and spoon up heaven.) The moist tres leches cake is covered in a silken meringue and served with dollops of lime custard and fresh mango salsa; the tender-crusted warm apple empañadas are doused with mole sauce and strewn with sugared pumpkin seeds. Pause for breath and take in the surroundings—the bright colors, the shimmering blue glass waterfall that is a design trademark of Rosa Mexicano interiors. Then consider the ice creams—like raspberry-rose with its exotic fragrance, the pungent coffee-Kailua, peanut crunch—available three at a time or as part of a humongous sundae that Jackie aptly described as "a party all by itself." Our sentiments exactly.

Note: At all locations, Rosa Mexicano celebrates the foods and traditions of Mexico with three annual festivals that include special menus and cooking demonstrations:

September–October: Chocolate Festival, at which the special dessert just might be layered chocolate cake with prickly pear, lime, and guanabana ice creams.

November: Day of the Dead with Oaxacan Flavors, featuring pumpkin-piloncillo crème brulee with Mexican chocolate sauce.

August: Ice Cream Festival, a chance to try avocado-honey ice cream, tamarind and lime sorbet, and much more.

Tres Leches Cake

It seems to be cropping up everywhere in endless variations, this cake soaked with three kinds of sweetened milks—evaporated, sweetened condensed, and sometimes cream. Often you find it with a meringue topping, sometimes chocolate, sometimes plain, but they're all called by the same name. We asked Roberto

Santibanez, former culinary director of **Rosa Mexicano**, what he knew of its origins. "Every Latin American country knows about it," he said, pointing out that it's become so popular that in Mexico City there are cake stores dedicated solely to tres leches. Santibanez believes that it was not originally a Latin recipe. Because tres leches cake is not remembered in Mexico before the 1950s or '60s, Santibanez suspects that the recipe may have been introduced by a condensed milk company around that time as a promotion. Wherever it came from, it caught on, appealing to the famous Latin sweet tooth, and today even upscale restaurants like Rosa Mexicano offer it. At the Lincoln Center location, tres leches is served in a chocolate-rum version topped with vanilla ice cream and served with sugared bananas. We discovered an excellent plain version, served simply with a cinnamon stick and fresh mint, at **Mexicana Mama** (525 Hudson St. bet. Charles and West 10th Sts., 212-924-4119), a tiny, very popular West Village restaurant, where you can order it at the bar or get it to go. **Itzocan Café** (438 East 9th St. bet. First Ave. and Ave. A, 212-677-5856) makes a super-moist tres leches cake enhanced with Mexican chocolate sauce. At **La Flor Bakery and Café** (53-02 Roosevelt Ave., in Queens, 718-426-8023), tres leches is made with creamy white frosting and is served with fresh fruit salsa. **Crema**'s version (111 West 17th St. bet. Sixth and Seventh Aves.; 212-691-4477) is served with mango syrup and dulce de leche ice cream.

sant ambroeus

✴ *259 West 4th Street bet. Charles and Perry Streets*
   PHONE: 212-604-9254

✴ *1000 Madison Avenue bet. 77th and 78th Streets*
   PHONE: 212-604-570-2211
   CREDIT CARDS: MC, V
   PRICE RANGE: gelati and pastries, $9
   WEB: www.santambroeus.com

Why is Sant Ambroeus spelled in that odd way? Glad you asked: It's the Milanese dialect for Sant'Ambrogio, that city's fourth century patron saint. So honored is he that the Milanese refer to themselves as "Ambrosiani." It's no wonder, then, that the Pauli family borrowed the sweet saint's name for their now legendary ice cream shop, which has been operating in Milan since 1936. Transposed to New York as a full-service (and super pricey) bistro-style restaurant in 1983, Sant Ambroeus remains famous for its pastries, desserts, and gelati. The more recently opened West Village location—our favorite—offers a suitably old-world sidewalk café at which to enjoy the famed cappuccino with breakfast cornetti, or, throughout the day, any one of the dozen irresistible confections always on the menu. The gorgeous Botticelli is a flower-shaped chocolate jewel—a feast for the eyes and the palate—filled with rich flourless chocolate sponge cake and dark chocolate mousse; bavarese combines delicate vanilla cream-filled chocolate cake with raspberry jelly; and the namesake Sant Ambroeus delivers an exquisite triple-threat chocolate punch in the form of sponge, crème brûlée, and ganache. Our Italian friend Anna-Teresa pronounced the tiramisu—classically composed of espresso-soaked *savoiardi* cookies and mascarpone cream—"buono." If you opt to sit inside for your dessert—expect to be accommodated off-peak, not during busy lunch and dinner hours—you'll be seated either at the bar, or at one of the cozy tables in a warmly decorated room complete with lacey café curtains, pink tablecloths, beaded hanging lamps, and Roman-striped upholstery on banquettes and chairs. Sant Ambroeus can be habit-forming. Once you've enjoyed the sweets you may be persuaded to think in terms of ambrosia.

~~~~~~

sarabeth's

　❋ *Hotel Wales, 1295 Madison Avenue bet. 92nd and 93rd Streets*
　　PHONE: 212-410-7335
　❋ *Whitney Museum of American Art, 945 Madison Avenue at 75th Street*
　　PHONE: 212-570-3670
　❋ *423 Amsterdam Avenue bet. 80th and 81st Streets*
　　PHONE: 212-496-6280
　　CREDIT CARDS: AmEx, MC, V
　　PRICE RANGE: $6.75–7.25
　　WEB: www.sarabeths.com
　　See also Chelsea Market page 35

Our favorite Sarabeth location is the Whitney because, frankly, it has the best art-celebrity watching—especially weekdays. You can depend on Sarabeth's baked goods and know you'll be getting a nice piece of chocolate mousse cake or a good vanilla bread pudding, strawberry shortcake, or Ciao Bella gelato with your coffee or tea, but you might also get a look at regulars like Yoko Ono or Chuck Close, who have been known to stop by. We also like the echo-y hum of the building that fills the air above our heads as we contemplate a show we might have just seen, or plan to see (you don't have to pay museum entry to go to Sarabeth's one flight down). You feel your dessert is a proper reward for having caught some culture and shocked a few brain cells out of torpor, even if you went no further than Calder's Circus, on permanent view in the lobby. NOTE: The museum is closed on Monday. Tues.–Fri. 11a.m.–3:45 p.m.; Sat.–Sun. 10 a.m.–4:30 p.m.

~~~~~~

seppi's

❉ *123 West 56th Street bet. Sixth and Seventh Avenues*
PHONE: 212-708-7444
CREDIT CARDS: AmEx, MC, V, Disc
PRICE RANGE: $7–11
WEB: www.parkermeridien.com

This is the kind of place you love to happen upon by accident, then sit in its cozy confines, congratulating yourself on your good fortune. That's just what we did on a rainy afternoon, stopping to chat with chef-owner Claude Alain Solliard, who was lunching late at the bar.

Newspapers at the door, mismatched old posters and prints adorning the pressed tin walls, blackboards with the specials and wines of the day, long hours (11:30 a.m. to 2 a.m.); all reflect the smiling Claude's commitment to establishing a haven where you can drop by, "be comfortable," linger, and order as little (or as much) as you choose. For desserts, that means much the same selection as you'd find at that little place you'd love to happen upon in Paris: tarte Tatin, crème brûlée aux noisette, soufflé au chocolat blanc and—the best seller among the regulars—the caramelized hot banana tart with molten chocolate.

The special prix fixe Sunday brunch is "inspired by chocolate," and includes such temptations as a chocolate mimosa and, for closure, an extravagant chocolate buffet.

norma's at the parker meridien

❊ *118 West 57th Street bet. Sixth and Seventh Avenues*
PHONE: 212-708-7460
CREDIT CARDS: AmEx, MC, V, Disc
PRICE RANGE: $6–15
WEB: www.parkermeridien.com

If you're an earlier bird than Seppi's 11:30 a.m. opening, the Parker Meridien, which shelters Seppi's, offers breakfast and brunch fare at Norma's that should jolt the sweetest tooth. Among the more fanciful temptations served in this sleekly modernist room: chocolate decadence french toast, the rich brioche slices cloaked in strawberries, pistachios, and chocolate sauce; mango papaya brown butter cinnamon flap jacks; caramelized chocolate banana waffle napoleon; raspberry risotto oatmeal; and Waz-Za, a waffle with fruit inside and out with a crunchy brûlée top. Norma's closes at 3 p.m.

serendipity 3

❊ *225 East 60th Street bet. Second and Third Avenues*
PHONE: 212-838-3531
CREDIT CARDS: AmEx, DC, Disc, MC, V
PRICE RANGE: "Frrrozen" hot chocolate, $8.50; desserts, $7–20 (banana split)
WEB: www.serendipity3.com

A chocoholic checkpoint for fifty years, Serendipity 3 serves up its famous "Frrrozen" hot chocolate in a warm, funky ambience that has charmed New Yorkers—celebrities and otherwise—since 1954. Served up in a mega-goblet with a pile of whipped cream and two straws, the slushy drink blends twelve kinds of super-delicious chocolate with cocoa powders, milk, sugar, and ice. The restaurant/gift shop also sells it in three different forms: as a packaged mix (just add milk, ice, and blend) that you can take home to maintain your chocolate high; as a mocha-colored lip gloss that smells great but is unflavored; and as bath and body gel (just don't squirt it on ice cream).

Serendipity 3's cachet among the sundae-seeking glitterati seems never to have lessened since Andy Warhol declared it his favorite sweet shop and Jackie Kennedy brought Caroline and John-John in for the famous foot-long hot dogs. The funky, ice cream parlor ambience, complete with Tiffany-style lampshades, continues to charm hordes of New Yorkers who go not just for the humongous drug store sundaes, banana splits, or lemon ice box pie, but also for hamburgers and vegetarian chili. There's a children's menu (as well as toys and other things for kids and grownups to buy on the way out) and a general atmosphere of fun being had by all. You're just not a New Yorker until you've been to Serendipity 3.

kid destinations

Most places in this book welcome kids. In general we've avoided destinations that are going to subject anybody—you or your children—to a lot of attitude or eye-rolling. (If you have any question about kid-friendliness, just call and ask.) But basically, our Best 50+ have been chosen with your own more—um—sophisticated adult sensibilities in mind. Unless you're prepping your child for early admission to Le Cordon Bleu, consider for places that put kids' enjoyment first.

Uppity Fudge, Chocolate Turtles, Brownie Splits, S'More Sundaes, and other kid-friendly delights are ready and waiting at **Divalicious Chocolate!** (365 Broome St., bet. Mott and Elizabeth Sts., 212-343-1243, www. divaliciouschocolate.com), where eponymous diva Jackie Gordon offers educational chocolate tastings, made-to-order parties, and, for the dippingest fun, a chocolate fountain (rentals available). At the Tex-Mex **Cowgirl Hall of Fame** (519 Hudson St. at 10th St., 212-633-1133, www.cowgirlnyc.com) kids can explore a Western mini-museum, displays of barbed wire, and a funky gift shop, while waiting for the famous trompe l'oeil ice cream baked potato: the potato's a cocoa-dusted chunk of ice cream, whipped cream stands in for sour cream, green-dyed chopped pecans are chives, and banana buttercream is the butter pat—hilariously funny if you're seven years old. At **Dylan's Candy Bar** (1011 Third Ave. at 60th St., 646-735-0078, www.dylanscandybar.com) kids flock down the gummi-bear-embedded staircase to a nirvana of sweets—over five thousand kinds—and a soda fountain, too. **Mars 2112** (1633 Broadway at 51st St., 212-582-2112, www.mars2112.com) provides a simulated trip to the Red Planet that can lead to an Earthling-friendly meal of chicken fingers and a three-scoop Polar Ice Caps sundae or Andromeda Apple Pie.

With older kids, teens, and you in mind, **Hard Rock Café** (1501 Broadway at 43rd St., 212-343-3355, www.hard rock.com) plays out the Times Square experience with down-home apple cobbler, a five-layer chocolate cake and, in a huge margarita glass, a hot fudge brownie sundae. Rock on! The baseball motifs at the **Brooklyn Diner** (212 West 57th St. bet. Seventh Ave. and Broadway, 212-977-1957; 155 West 43rd St. bet. Broadway and Sixth Ave, 212-265-5400, www.brooklyndiner.com) will delight young sluggers, who can cap off the famous fifteen-bite hot dog with a two-kid-sized chocolate fudge sundae or a gooey, monster slab of the diner's iconic Strawberry Blond cheesecake. The Willy Wonka-ish atmosphere at **Max Brenner—Chocolate by the Bald Man** (841 Broadway bet. 13th and 14th Sts., 646-467-8801; 141 Second Avenue at 9th St., 212-388-0030; www.maxbrenner.com) is craftily designed to charm kids of all ages, for whom the wacky desserts and "concoctions" on the multi-multi-multi-page menu are just part of the shenanigans. Bring Arlo and Isadora for the popsicle fondue while you enjoy any one of the perfectly good chocolate drinks in a "hug mug," or a chocolate-smothered banana split waffle, which should keep you grounded for the trip home. At **Petite Abeille** (www.petiteabeille.com for all locations), the little bee cartoons never fail to enchant children and their parents, who come for the hot chocolate and the Belgian waffles a la mode.

Ice cream shops not to be missed include the long-running **Chinatown Ice Cream Factory** (65 Bayard St. bet. Elizabeth and Mott Sts., 212-608-4170, www. chinatownicecreamfactory.com) with its weird and wonderful flavors and bright yellow dragon T-shirt—always available in kid sizes, and **Brooklyn Ice Cream Factory**

(1 Old Fulton St. at Water St., Brooklyn, 718-246-3963) located in a former fireboat house in a little park with a view of Manhattan. Strollers advisable for the long walk from the subway—the superlative hot fudge makes it all worthwhile.

Kids love to make their own desserts and confections, and the learning experience doesn't get any better or more fun than at **Candy Camp**, held at master pastry chef Jehengir Meta's Graffiti, (224 East 10th St. at First Ave., 212-464-7743). On the first Saturday of every month from 10 a.m. to 11:30 a.m., chef Meta welcomes children ages 4 to 14, accompanied by a parent; $40 up. Baking lessons are also the highpoint of kids' birthday parties at specialty bakery **Tribeca Treats** (94 Reade St. at Church St., 212-571-0500, www.tribeca-treats.com) where children three and up produce their own cupcakes, cookies, cookie pizzas, and chocolate as part of the guided festivities. On Sundays, owner Rachel Thebault makes the bakery available for parties of up to twelve children and their parents (90-minute parties cost $750) that include—along with baking activities—food, decorated birthday cakes, games, stories, and party favors. Coffee is available for the grownups too.

While **Cupcake Café at Books of Wonder** (18 West 18th St. at Fifth Ave., 212-465-1530) may not offer baking lessons, it does afford kids and their parents the rare opportunity to browse through children's books, either before or after (wash hands, please) enjoying one of this bakery's gorgeously decorated cupcakes—buttercream artistry gone technicolor. For more kid-friendly destinations see also **Elephant and Castle, Columbus Bakery, Edgar's Café, Good Enough to Eat, Magnolia Bakery, Podunk, Sarabeth's,** and **Yura.**

strip house

❖ *13 East 12th Street bet. Fifth Avenue and University Place*

PHONE: 212-328-0000

CREDIT CARDS: AmEx, MC, V, Disc

PRICE RANGE: $8–16

WEB: www.theglaziergroup.com

Go for the chocolate cake. We're not the first ones to say it, nor the last, as long as chef René Luger remains in charge. This is not a molten chocolate cake, chocolate mousse cake, chocolate decadence, or gateau au chocolat. It's the chocolate layer cake that is the emotional equivalent for many Americans of Proust's madeleine, with alternating layers of chocolate sponge cake and thick, dark chocolate custard under an even richer chocolate frosting. In this case, twenty-four thin layers stand so tall and moist that each slice trembles when you touch it with your fork.

Strip House occupies the site where Asti's waiters once burst into song at the drop of an ice cube. The Italian songsters are gone, but Strip House pays homage to their memory with dense hangings of Asti's photos of mostly bygone celebrities against the red-flocked wallpaper. There are also some vintage photos of flirtatious bare-bosomed belles of the 1920s, giving the darkly lit room a raffish look.

For dessert alone, you'll probably be seated up front in the bar and lounge. And, of course, you can choose among René Luger's other specialties, like the eye-opening Clou du Mont coffee crème brûlée, served with a pot of Clou du Mont Vintage 2002 coffee. Or a warm crèpe soufflé with vanilla ice cream melting inside it, drenched with mandarin oranges and blackberries.

Go for the chocolate cake.

sullivan street bakery

✳ *533 West 47th Street at Tenth Avenue*
PHONE: 212-265-5580
CREDIT CARDS: MC, V
PRICE RANGE: bomboloni $2; fruit tart $4; tart Tatin
slices $2.50, whole $28
WEB: www.sullivanstreetbakery.com

When Jim Lahey and Monica Von Thun Calderón ended their partnership, Lahey took the bakery name to this Hell's Kitchen location, from which he continues to supply breads to hundreds of restaurants around town. He has eighty-sixed the crostatas, but upped the store's dessert quotient with tender, crumble-topped, seasonal fruit tarts packed with Greenmarket apples, pears, or blueberries; bomboloni, Italian custard-filled donuts that explode at first bite; warm tart Tatin made with deeply caramelized golden delicious apples; and stecca, bread strips baked with savory, but sometimes sweet—toppings, like concord grape in the fall. Mainstays include tortino de cioccolato, with its soft crunch and delicate melting texture; biscotti, including crumbs for sprinkling on ice cream; and airy, crunchy cookies called ossi de morti, because they actually resemble bones.

grandaisy bakery

✳ *73 Sullivan Street bet. Spring and Broome Streets*
✳ *176 West 72nd Street at Amsterdam Avenue*
PHONE: 212-334-9435 (both locations)
CREDIT CARDS: AmEx, MC, V, Disc; $5 minimum
PRICE RANGE: tarts $3.50–4; whole crostata $28; whole cakes about $32
WEB: www.grandaisybakery.com

Grandaisy occupies the site of the original Sullivan Street Bakery, where Monica Von Thun Calderón continues to supply baked goods of substantially the same fine quality and type: artisanal breads, thin-crust pizzas, and of course desserts that made the original famous, including fruit tarts and cookies; tortino de cioccolato; crostatas filled with home-made jam; and luscious cakes—including ricotta cheesecake—all made in the unadorned, authentic Italian style. Holiday specials include pumpkin pie, a Christmas panetonne, and for Easter the dove-shaped Columba cake.

union square café

❖ *21 East 16th Street at Union Square West*
PHONE: 212-243-4020
CREDIT CARDS: AmEx, MC, V, Disc
PRICE RANGE: $9.50
WEB: www.unionsquarecafe.com

How much do you need to know? Now nearing the quarter-century mark, the standards at Union Square Café—the first of restaurateur Danny Meyer's fabled Manhattan dining desti-nations—are as high as they ever were, and its patrons as loyal as the queen's corgis. The secret for avoiding the reser-vations telephone logjam: don't call ahead. They don't accept reservations for sitting at the bar, anyway. All it takes is a bit of smart timing to claim an empty seat. Your only frustration is having to choose from among pastry chef Stacy Klein's good-as-they-get, ever-changing, daily delights.

Perhaps it's the chocolate napoleon with salted caramel mousse and devil's food cake? Or a Greenmarket peach tart with toasted hazelnut ice milk? Depending on seasonal produce it could be an autumn concord grape panna cotta with peanut-butter and crispy peanut tuile. Of course, you probably can't do better than the café's perennial banana tart with honey-vanilla ice cream and macadamia brittle. Then again, with the Union Square Greenmarket just steps from the kitchen, you might never again have the chance to savor one of the day's flights of imagination. Ah, the problems life can bring.

a glossary of dessert terms

Whether reading a menu or making a choice at a fancy pastry shop or down-home bakery, you're bound to encounter some of the following words and terms.

apfelstrudel: apple strudel; see strudel.

assiette: the French word for "plate"; an assortment of foods of a particular type arranged on a plate, as in "lemon assiette" describing a dessert of several lemon-flavored items.

baba: usually a small individual yeast-risen cake flavored with rum after baking.

baked alaska: a hot-and-cold dessert in which ice cream is surrounded by hot meringue on a base of liqueur-soaked sponge cake.

bavarese: Italian for Bavarian cream; see Bavarois.

bavarian cream: see Bavarois.

bavarois (bav-ar-WA): French term for a cold egg custard dessert mixed with whipped cream and flavored and set in a mold.

belle-helene: a cold dessert of poached pears served with vanilla ice cream and hot chocolate sauce.

biscotti: in Italian the word means "baked twice" and describes the way in which these crisp, nutty cookies are made in dozens of varieties; delicious with coffee or dunked in sweet wine.

bûche de noël: a rolled Christmas cake filled and spread with chocolate or mocha buttercream that is made to look like a log and decorated with meringue mushrooms.

gâteau (ga-TOH): the French word for "cake."

cannoli: the plural of cannolo ("cannon"), a pastry tube filled with ricotta cream, the classic Sicilian dessert.

caramel: the deep golden-brown syrup that results when sugar is cooked and caramelized.

cassata: a rich Sicilian cake, usually sponge cake, filled with ricotta cream (like cannoli cream), covered with white sugar icing or marzipan and decorated with candied fruit.

chantilly (SHAHN-tee-ee): sweetened whipped cream; also *crème Chantilly*.

charlotte: a dessert made in a mold lined with ladyfingers, filled with fruit or other flavored custard, mousse, or bavarois, and served unmolded.

choux pastry: a pastry used for making éclairs and cream-puffs that puffs out during baking and is then filled with cream or custard; also *pâte à choux*.

clafoutis (kla-FOO-tee): a French-style cake made by placing fruit (traditionally cherries) in a buttered dish, pouring in a pancake-like batter, and baking it; often served warm.

chiboust: a type of custard pastry cream, usually vanilla-flavored, that is blended while warm with stiffly beaten egg whites.

crème brûlée: a chilled cream-based custard dessert topped with a layer of usually brown sugar which is caramelized into a sweet brittle crust before serving.

crêpe: a thin pancake made in a frying (or crêpe pan). Sweet crêpes are often made with vanilla-flavored sugar, filled with creams or custard and served with powdered sugar. The famous crêpe suzette is flavored with orange or tangerine and Grand Marnier or Curacao liqueur and served *en flambé* tableside.

croquembouche: usually a fancy, towering presentation composed of piled creampuffs stuck together with a caramel glaze; popular as a wedding cake.

crostata: a flat, shortbread type of Italian pastry, filled with fruit puree, usually raspberry or apricot.

dacquoise: a cake made from layers of hazelnut-flavored meringues filled with whipped cream.

éclair: finger- or log-shaped pastry filled with cream and glazed.

financier (fee-NAHN-cee-ay): a small, rectangular almond-flavored sponge cake, supposedly resembling a gold brick, hence the name.

flan: a caramelized egg custard.

fraisier (FRAY-zee-ay): a fancy cake made with fresh strawberries and strawberry jam.

frangipane (FRAN-zhuh-pan): almond cream.

galette: a flat, round cake, savory or sweet; sometimes a type of French tart.

ganache (gan-ASCH): a mixture of bittersweet chocolate and cream used as icing or filling in a cake or pastry.

gianduja (zhan-DU-ya): chocolate flavored with hazelnuts or almonds.

key lime: a variety of lime that is smaller, and more mild, than the common Persian lime, and more yellow than green.

kouing-aman: a large flat Breton cake made of buttery, cream-enriched bread dough and topped with caramelized sugar.

kugelhopf: an Austrian yeast cake baked in a crown-like mold and filled with raisins, currants, and sometimes fruit and nuts.

kulfi: a type of dense Indian ice cream made with a cream reduction.

linzertorte: an Austrian shortbread pastry flavored with ground almonds and grated lemon rind and topped with raspberry jam; named for the town of Linz, Austria.

macaroon: a round cookie, crunchy outside and soft inside, made with ground almonds, or almond paste, sugar, and egg whites; coconut macaroons substitute coconut for almonds.

madeleine: a small sponge cake, made in a seashell-shaped mold, usually flavored with lemon or orange; made famous by Marcel Proust in *Remembrance of Things Past*, in which the taste of the cake evoked memories.

megeve (meh-ZHEV): a cake made of crunchy white vanilla meringue, chocolate mousse, and ganache, topped with chocolate glaze.

meringue: egg whites stiffly beaten with sugar.

meyer lemon: a variety of lemon whose juice is considerably sweeter than that of regular lemons.

mille-feuille (mee-FOY): a napoleon; a small rectangular pastry made of multiple layers of puff pastry filled with cream mousseline (a pastry cream with twenty percent Chantilly whipped cream) and iced with royal icing or fondant.

mont blanc (monte bianco, Italian): named for the alpine peak that stands between France and Italy, a pastry claimed by both countries; composed of a mound of sweetened, vanilla-flavored chestnut puree that is "snow-capped" with whipped cream or Chantilly cream; often prepared on a tart-crust base. The Italian version is further flavored with brandy or Cognac; the French version is made in an almond tart shell filled with vanilla meringue, Chantilly cream, wild rose petal puree, and topped with piped chestnut cream.

mousse: a light, fluffy, cream-based mixture flavored with fruit puree or chocolate.

napoleon: see *mille-feuille*.

opera: a rich French pastry composed of thin, alternating layers of almond sponge cake, mocha coffee cream, and dark chocolate ganache, topped with dark chocolate glaze and often decorated with edible gold leaf.

panettone: a sweet Italian Christmas cake made from a rich yeast dough containing raisins and candied fruit.

pannacotta: Italian for "cooked cream"; a heated, eggless cream made in a mold, much lighter than baked custard.

parisbrest (pa-ree-BREST): a wheel-shaped éclair filled with praline-flavored cream and sprinkled with almonds, created in 1891 to commemorate the famous Paris-Brest bicycle race. *Parisnice* is a variation without almonds.

pavlova: a dessert claimed by both Australia (some say the national dish) and New Zealand in which a soft-centered meringue is filled with a cream-and-passionfruit mixture; named for the Russian ballerina Anna Pavlova.

pithivier (pee-tee-VYAY): a round tart of puff-pastry filled with almond cream (*frangipane*).

plated: several different items arranged on a plate, as in "plated dessert."

pound cake: a loaf cake made with equal parts flour, sugar, butter, and eggs.

praline: a crunchy, candy-like preparation made of crushed almonds and/or hazelnuts and caramelized sugar, used as a garnish or filling in desserts.

profiterole: a cream-puff dessert filled with cream or ice cream and often served with hot chocolate sauce.

religieuse (ruh-lee-JYUZ): usually a small pastry made of chocolate éclairs arranged in a pyramid, piped with mocha buttercream, whose color is said to resemble the homespun habit worn by French nuns, hence the name.

sablé (SA-blay): a French butter and sugar cookie with a "sandy" texture.

sacher torte: rich chocolate Viennese layer cake filled with apricot jam and coated with chocolate glaze, always served with whipped cream; named for the famed Sacher Hotel in Vienna, where it was created in the mid-nineteenth century.

sabayon: see zabaglione.

saint-honoré: a French cake, named for the patron saint of bakers and pastry cooks, made with a shortcrust base, a caramel-glazed puff pastry on top, and a garnish of cream puffs arranged in a ring to form a sort of crown. The whole thing is filled with cream.

savoiardi: Italian-style ladyfingers, the sponge-cake-like cookies often used to make tiramisu.

semifreddo: a "half-frozen" mousse-like mixture not made in an ice cream maker but in a mold in the freezer; semifreddi have an airy texture as whipped cream or meringue.

sfogliatelle (sfol-ya-TEL-eh): a Neapolitan flaky pastry in the shape of a clamshell filled with a ricotta/semolina mixture.

soufflé: a light dessert containing cream, sugar, and egg yolks into which beaten whites are folded causing the mixture to puff up during baking.

streusel: the crumbly topping, comprised of flour, sugar and butter, and sometimes spices and nuts, sprinkled on cakes and pastries.

strudel: a pastry made of sheets of very thin dough filled usually with fruit (apple is most popular) or sweetened cheese and rolled, baked and served cut in slices; a specialty of Austria and Germany. (The word means "eddy" or "whirlpool" in German.)

struffoli: Italian Christmas pastry comprised of tiny, fried balls of dough that are arranged in a wreath shape and coated with honey or caramel.

tarte Tatin: an apple tart in which the apples are cooked "upside down" with the fruit at the bottom of the pan in butter and sugar and the pastry on top; served inverted so the caramelized apples are on top; named after the Tatin sisters from the Loire region of France; also made with pears; first served at Maxim's in Paris.

tiramisu: a rich coffee-flavored dessert from Treviso, near Venice, consisting of ladyfingers (or sponge cake) soaked with espresso syrup and brandy, layered with a mascarpone-whipped cream mixture and topped with whipped cream and cocoa powder or shaved chocolate; there are hundreds of variations.

torta: Italian word for "cake."

tuile (tweel): a thin, delicate cookie that is shaped while still hot.

vacherin (vash-RAN): a dessert made of rings of meringue piped on top of each other to form a shell, which is then filled with ice cream or whipped cream and sometimes garnished with candied fruit; named for a round white cheese of the same name, which it resembles.

viennoiserie: at a French bakery, non-bread items such as croissants, brioche, and the like.

zabaglione; **zabaione** (zag-bal-YOH-neh): a foamy Italian dessert in which egg yolks, sweet wine, and sugar are whisked together over low heat to make a light custard; in French, sabayon.

zuppa inglese (zoopa-een-GLAZE-a): literally "English soup"; an Italian dessert, similar to English trifle, made from rum-moistened sponge cake layered with pastry cream, often decorated with chocolate shavings and candied fruit.

favorite neighborhood bakeries and cafés

CHELSEA

La Bergamote
169 Ninth Avenue at 20th Street
PHONE: 212-627-9010
French pastries, with an emphasis on mousse cakes, in an appealing café setting.

Billy's Bakery
184 Ninth Avenue bet. 21st and 22nd Streets
PHONE: 212-647-9956
WEB: www.billysbakerynyc.com
Old-fashioned cakes, pies, and cupcakes in a bright country-store setting. Banana cream more than stands out.

CHINATOWN

Egg Custard King Café
76 Mott Street bet. Canal and Bayard Streets
PHONE: 212-226-8208
Mini custard tarts are $.75 each. The "crème brûlée" variety, warm with caramelized top is the best of the flavors and well worth the trip.

Cecel Crêpe Café

135 First Avenue bet. St. Mark's Place and 9th Street
PHONE: 212-460-5102
A warm, freshly made crêpe is folded and filled to the brim with rich cream, fresh fruits, chocolate and the like, for a sweet-wrap kind of dessert experience.

Moishe's Kosher Bake Shop

115 Second Avenue bet. 6th and 7th Streets
PHONE: 212-505-8555
504 Grand Street bet. Columbia and Willets Streets
PHONE: 212-673-5832
Hamantaschen, rugelach, strudel, and other kosher sweets that East Village regulars swear by.

Panya

10 Stuyvesant Street bet. Third Avenue and 9th Street
PHONE: 212-777-1930
Japanese green-tea and mochi cookies, sweets and drinks, like green tea au lait, or iced yuzu tea with a citrus-y tang.

Tarallucci e Vino

163 First Avenue at 10th Street
PHONE: 212-388-1190
15 East 18th Street bet. Fifth Avenue and Broadway
PHONE: 212-228-5400

A cozy café serving excellent panini, and a large selection of pastries and dolci, including tarallucci, the Abruzzese semolina cookies made for dunking in vino.

Bouley Bakery/Market

130 West Broadway at Duane Street

Phone: 212-608-5363

WEB: www.davidbouley.com

Nestled among the luxurious French pastries and fruit tarts, you'll find one of the city's best brownies and utterly munchable peanut butter cookies.

Bubby's

120 Hudson Street at North Moore Street

PHONE: 212-219-0666

WEB: www.bubbys.com

A longtime family-friendly restaurant/bakery known for overstuffed fruit pies, cream pies, and tasty layer cakes—red velvet and spicy carrot stand out.

Duane Park Patisserie

179 Duane Street bet. Greenwich and Harrison Streets

PHONE: 212-274-8447

An out-of-the-way little gem with beautifully decorated and delicious butter cookies, outstanding cakes, an awesome lemon tart, a perfect little brownie and special-order cakes all courtesy of Madeline Lanciani.

Tribeca Treats

94 Reade Street at Church Street

PHONE: 212-571-0500

WEB: www.tribecatreats.com

A bakery with eighteen different "specialty" cakes and cupcakes of high quality, with a special interest in children's parties, baking lessons included. (See page 95.)

Cupcake Café at Books of Wonder

18 West 18th Street bet. 5th and 6th Avenues

PHONE: 212-465-1530

WEB: www.cupcakecafe.com

The multicolored frostings on the cupcakes are gaudy delights for the sticky-fingered set, and their grownups, too.

Tisserie

857 Broadway at 17th Street

PHONE: 212-463-0847

WEB: www.tisserie.com

Put together your own tasting party with affordable mini Euro-style pastries ($.75; $1.50), excellent fruit tarts, mousse cakes, financiers, brownies, and cookies.

GREENWICH VILLAGE

Beard Papa

740 Broadway at Astor Place; see website for all other locations

PHONE: 212-353-8888

WEB: www.muginohousa.com

Luscious Japanese cream puffs, puff-pastry shells baked on site and filled on demand in nine flavors. See also Choux Factory page 117.

Dean & DeLuca

75 University Place at 10th Street

PHONE: 212-473-1908

Not the SoHo gourmet madhouse, but a peaceful sit-down café in which to enjoy the good-quality pastries for which

D&D is known, although without some of downtown's high-end specialties.

Magnolia Bakery

401 Bleecker Street at 11th Street
PHONE: 212-462-2572
The limos still wait curbside for their cupcake-mad, banana-pudding craving, layer-cake loving clients to emerge from this tiny bakery that is approaching landmark status.

Marquet Patisserie

15 East 12th Street bet. Fifth Avenue and University Place
PHONE: 212-229-9313
Charming patisserie/café whose specialty is the fraisier, the prettiest, green-iced strawberry cake in town.
OTHER LOCATIONS: 221 Court St. at Baltic St., Brooklyn, 718-852-9267; 680 Fulton St., bet. S. Elliott Pl. and S. Portland Ave., Brooklyn, 718-596-2018

Patisserie Claude

187 West 4th Street bet. Sixth and Seventh Avenues
PHONE: 212-255-5911
Grumpy Claude might hang up on you, but he makes excellent, inexpensive tarts and cakes.

LOWER EAST SIDE

Babycakes

248 Broome Street bet. Orchard and Ludlow Streets
PHONE: 212-677-5047
WEB: www.babycakesnyc.com
Vegan-central for moist cupcakes, loaf cakes, cookies, cinnamon buns, and more. (See page 84.)

The Doughnut Plant

379 Grand Street bet. Essex and Norfolk Streets

PHONE: 212-505-3700

WEB: www.doughnutplant.com

Mark Israel's popular, oversized doughnuts have a cult following (also available at Dean & DeLuca).

How Sweet It Is

157 Allen Street at Rivington Street

PHONE: 212-777-0418

WEB: www.howsweetitispastry.com

Imaginative, finely crafted pastries: mini versions of bananas foster, minus the flambé; mellow goat cheesecake in *kataifi* nests; lemony cheese puffs; just to name a few.

Sugar Sweet Sunshine

126 Rivington Street at Norfolk Street

PHONE: 212-995-1960

WEB: www.sugarsweetsunshine.com

Hurry on down for the creamy banana pudding, chocolate bombe chocolate pudding, vanilla cupcakes, and seasonal pumpkin cupcakes with cream cheese icing.

SOHO

Grandaisy

73 Sullivan Street bet. Spring and Broome Streets

PHONE: 212-334-9435

WEB: www.grandaisybakery.com

See page 99.

MIDTOWN EAST

Buttercup Bake Shop
973 Second Avenue bet. 51st and 52nd Streets
PHONE: 212-350-4144
Cupcakes and more courtesy of an alumna of Magnolia Bakery.

MIDTOWN WEST/HELL'S KITCHEN

Choux Factory
316 West 23rd Street bet. 8th & 9th Avenues
PHONE: 212-627-4318
1685 First Avenue bet. 87th and 88th Streets
PHONE: 212-289-2023
Filled-to-order cream puffs in flavors such as vanilla,
chocolate, green tea, lemon meringue, and strawberry.
Kona coffee, too.

Cupcake Café
522 Ninth Avenue at 39th Street
PHONE: 212-465-1530
Also at Books of Wonder, 18 West 18th Street
PHONE: 212-465-1530
Funky little takeout bakery with a surprise: amazingly
decorated cakes for all occasions.

Bis.Co.Latte
677 10th Avenue at 47th Street
PHONE: 212-581-3900
WEB: www.biscolatte.com
The best biscotti in the city, we say, with a zillion varieties
baked fresh daily, and ready to enjoy in a charming café
setting, where gelati, muffins, and frittatas are also available.

Certé

20 West 55th Street bet. Fifth and Sixth Avenues

PHONE: 212-397-2020

Along with a mile-long menu of savories, Certé provides the fashionable Midtown crowd with everything from black-and-whites to tropical panna cotta and Valrhona brownies.

Ruby et Violette

457 West 50th Street bet. Ninth and Tenth Avenues

PHONE: 212-582-6720

www.rubyetviolette.com

Chocolate chip cookies in more than forty varieties: brown-sugary chewy masterpieces, loaded with chunks of semi-sweet chocolate.

Sullivan Street Bakery

533 West 47th Street

PHONE: 212 265 5580

WEB: www.sullivanstreetbakery.com

See page 99.

UPPER EAST SIDE

Andre's Café

1631 Second Avenue bet. 84th and 85th Streets

PHONE: 212-327-1105

WEB: www.andrescafenyc.com

Authentic Hungarian strudel—apple, cherry, and cherry-cheese stand out—and don't miss the *palacsinta* (apricot-and nut-filled crêpes).

Glaser's Bake Shop

1670 First Avenue bet. 87th and 88th Streets

PHONE: 212-289-2562

WEB: www.glasersbakeshop.com

Old-fashioned down-home baked goods since 1902.

Lady M

41 East 78th Street near Madison Avenue

PHONE: 212-452-2222

WEB: www.ladymconfections.com

Gâteaux for a château: twenty-layer mille crêpe; couronne du chocolate; tarte au fruit; and a $70 *New-Yorkaise* cheese-cake (you have to buy the whole thing). Slices for all else, $7.

Melange Food Fair

1277 First Avenue bet. 68th and 69th Streets

PHONE: 212-535-7773

Honey-drenched Middle Eastern pastries made by the Egyptian-born El-Naggar brothers.

Two Little Red Hens

1652 Second Avenue bet. 85th and 86th Streets

PHONE: 212-452-0476

1112 Eighth Avenue bet. 11th and 12th Streets, Brooklyn

PHONE: 718-499-8108

Worth the trip for pudding-filled, fudge-topped Brooklyn Blackout cupcakes, hazelnut velvet cake, and New York-style cheesecake.

William Greenberg Jr. Desserts

1000 Madison Avenue bet. 82nd and 83rd Streets

PHONE: 212-744-0304

Venerable old-time chocolate cake source.

Yura & Company

1624/1659 Third Avenue at 93rd Street

1292 Madison Avenue at 92nd Street

PHONE: 212-860-8060

At Third Avenue, a gleaming white, loft-style open-kitchen, popular with after-schoolers and their moms for cupcakes, cookies, tea cakes and more; at Madison Avenue, sit-down café dining with the same good pastries.

UPPER WEST SIDE

Levain Bakery

167 West 74th Street bet. Columbus and Amsterdam Avenues

PHONE: 212-874-6080

The biggest dang cookies in town—weigh 'em. Six ounces a piece, and the chocolate chip is a three-mealer.

Margot Patisserie

2109 Broadway at 74th Street

PHONE: 212-721-0076

1212 Lexington Avenue bet. 83rd and 84th Streets

PHONE: 212-772-6064

In the French style, light and lovely pastries and cookies.

Silver Moon Bakery

2740 Broadway at 105th Street

PHONE: 212-866-4717

Owner Judith Norell, formerly a harpsichordist, sometimes hosts musical events at this place popular with Columbia students known for great artisanal bread, pastries, and cookies.

Zabar's

2245 Broadway bet. 80th and 81st Streets

PHONE: 212-787-2000

Home-baked strudels—apple, apricot, cherry cheese, chocolate cheese, pineapple cheese—at only $4.99 are reason enough to make a special trip to the great market.

BROOKLYN

Boerum Hill

One Girl Cookies

68 Dean Street at Smith Street

PHONE: 212-675-4996

WEB: www.onegirlcookies.com

Teeny tiny cookies, lovely to look at and gone in one or two bites; we love Lucia (caramel shortbread), chocolate-ganache Juliette, and orange-butter Sadie.

Prospect Heights

Joyce Bakeshop

646 Vanderbilt Avenue bet. Park and Prospect Places

PHONE: 718-623-7470

WEB: www.joycebakeshop.com

Master baker Joyce Quitasol turns out fresh pastries, elegant fruit tarts, cupcakes, layer cakes, and seasonal specialties including adorably iced holiday cookies.

Red Hook

Baked
359 Van Brunt Street at Dykeman Street
PHONE: 718-222-0345
WEB: www.baked.com
Try a slice of Red Hook Red Hot (red-velvet cake with cinnamon buttercream topped with candied red hots), or Sweet and Salty (chocolate cake with salty caramel-chocolate ganache topped with fleur de sel), just two reasons to make the subway-bus expedition.

Dumbo

Almondine
85 Water Street at Plymouth Street
PHONE: 718-797-5026
Flaky croissants, classic French pastries, homemade ice creams and sorbets in a cozy café setting, all just a stone's throw from Jacques Torres.

Park Slope

Sweet Melissa Patisserie
175 Seventh Avenue bet. First and Second Streets
PHONE: 718-502-9153
WEB: www.sweetmelissapatisserie.com
Bread pudding cake with raspberry sauce, oh yes; lemon mascarpone cheesecake, umm; chocolate-cherry cookies, more please; and lots more at this mommy-friendly bakery-café.

Trois Pommes

260 Fifth Avenue at Garfield Place

PHONE: 718-230-3119

WEB: www.troispommespatisserie.com

The Mostess cupcake with thick chocolate icing and espresso cream filling; the honey lavender ice cream; the cherry peach tart; and the key lime pie with lime-scented whipped cream are just a few reasons to visit Emily Isaac's charming retro bakery.

index
by name

new york's 50+ best places to enjoy dessert

new york's 50+ best places to enjoy dessert

index
by neighborhood

new york's 50+ best places to enjoy dessert

new york's 50+ best places to enjoy dessert